THE
ART
OF
STAYING
WELL
IN AN
UPTIGHT
WORLD

THE ART OF STAYING WELL IN AN UPTIGHT WORLD

Dr. Ken Olson

OLIVER NELSON

A Division of Thomas Nelson Publishers
Nashville

To my wife Jeannie,
who has stayed by me
all these years.

For better for worse,
For richer for poorer,
In sickness and in health,
To love and to cherish,
Till death us do part.

PUBLISHER'S NOTE: This book is intended for general preventive health care information only and is not intended to supplant medical advice, diagnosis, or treatment by a personal physician. Readers are urged to consult their personal physicians regarding illness, injury, and nutrition/nutritional supplements or before using any physical procedure.

Published in Nashville, Tennessee, by Oliver-Nelson Books, a division of Thomas Nelson, Inc., Publishers, and distributed in Canada by Lawson Falle, Ltd., Cambridge, Ontario.

Scripture quotations are from THE NEW KING JAMES VERSION. Copyright © 1979, 1980, 1982, Thomas Nelson, Inc., Publishers.

Verse marked TLB is taken from *The Living Bible,* copyright 1971 by Tyndale House Publishers, Wheaton, IL. Used by permission.

Printed in the United States of America.

ISBN 0-8407-9093-7

1 2 3 4 5 6 — 94 93 92 91 90 89

CONTENTS

Acknowledgments vii
1. The Art of Staying Well in an Uptight World 9
2. The Anatomy of Stress 22
3. The Healing Warriors Within 37
4. How to Prevent Coronary Heart Disease 52
5. The Ugly Face of Pain 72
6. Emotions and Your Health 92
7. The Healing Mind 123
8. Spiritually Alive and Healthy 147
9. It's All a Matter of Style—Life-Style 173

ACKNOWLEDGMENTS

A very special thanks to Eileen Roth for the art work done for the cover. The cover is a Photostration, which is a technique combining black and white photography with oil illustration. Photostration is trademarked by Eileen Roth, a Phoenix resident who was raised and trained in New York. This technique has been used in many applications in commercial and fine art.

Thanks also to Alan Roth for his cover design and production.

I would like to thank Marian Johnson, who is able to read my penmanship and thus make possible a typed manuscript.

And I would like to express my gratitude to Lila Empson, senior editor for Oliver-Nelson, for all her help in editing this book.

CHAPTER ONE

THE ART OF STAYING WELL IN AN UPTIGHT WORLD

When I wrote *The Art of Hanging Loose in an Uptight World* in 1973, I didn't think the world could get more uptight. I was wrong. Remember, that's when the Arabs drastically shut down our oil supply, and there were long, frustrating lines of motorists waiting for gas and hoping the filling station wouldn't run out of gasoline. In Arizona we even had some shout-outs among uptight people waiting for gasoline.

Now we have plenty of gasoline with the result that the streets in our major cities and the freeways are jammed with bumper-to-bumper traffic. People are so uptight that for many of them the greatest source of stress in life is not on the job, but in the traffic jams going to and from work. In Los Angeles the situation has gotten so tense that people are being shot and killed while driving on the freeway.

How uptight *is* our world? Let's take a look at vacations, for example. One of the time-honored ways to reduce stress has been to take a vacation and get away from it all. Well, in the past few years even these opportunities for relaxation have been beset by stressful circumstances, anxious moments, and potential danger.

9

In 1983, my wife, Jeannie, and I took a dream-of-a-lifetime vacation on the Royal Cruise Line through the Scandinavian countries to Leningrad, Russia. One afternoon, about five o'clock, I went out on deck to stretch my legs, and right beside our ship was a Russian freighter, dangerously close. I leaned closer to take a picture just as the Russian freighter turned in front of our ship in an attempt to cause a collision. In the nick of time, our captain gave orders to swerve our ship, thus narrowly avoiding the impending disaster. The next day, about the same time, the Russian freighter appeared. This time our captain came to a complete stop and waited until the Russian freighter sailed on ahead.

Tourists have been on airplanes that have been blown up or hijacked; they have been taken as hostages, beaten up, and murdered. Even one Italian cruise ship was hijacked. Terrorist bombs have killed and wounded tourists in airports, hotels, and restaurants. Yet all we tourists want is a nice, peaceful vacation to have some fun and reduce the stress in our lives.

I had not taken a vacation for three years since that cruise. Jeannie and I talked about going back to Europe, but we were very concerned about terrorists' attacks there. We even thought of dressing like Arabs to reduce the risk of being targets for terrorists, but having to take such precautions would certainly not contribute to a feeling of relaxation and enjoyment.

So we decided, Why not go to the peaceful, friendly islands of Fiji in the South Pacific? We had been there before and found the Fijian people to be quite hospitable. We made our reservations for Fiji—only to have a military coup of the government cause us to cancel our trip to the not-so-peaceful islands.

We do live in an uptight world. It's a time of crisis, change, turmoil, and fear. Most of us have lived our lives under the shadow of death from thermonuclear extinction. Now another "bomb"—AIDS—has exploded with deadly consequences on planet earth. The fear of AIDS is rampant throughout the world because it is a fatal disease with no cure. In fact, the epidemic is so widespread and so lethal that some experts are comparing it to the Black Death that killed a quarter of Europe's population in the fourteenth century. World public health officials estimate that before the disease has run its course, about one hundred million people will die from AIDS worldwide. That is as many people as those who died in all the wars and concentration camps of the twentieth century.[1]

The AIDS plague, to a large degree, is preventable. If people, mostly homosexuals, would stop having anal intercourse and drug addicts would stop shooting dope, especially with dirty needles, the AIDS epidemic could, in time, be stopped. In the late sixties and early seventies I ran an outpatient drug treatment center in Phoenix. I remember talking with a junky about the real danger of getting hepatitis from passing the same dirty needle around to other junkies in a "shooting gallery." The junky replied, "Doc, we try to be careful and make sure that the yellowest one gets the needle last."

These days it is difficult to stay healthy in our uptight world. I believe that 70 percent to 80 percent of the people going to physicians are ill not because of an infectious disease caused by a germ, but because of the wear and tear of too much chronic stress in their lives. There is no pill to cure their sickness, no surgical procedure that will remove its root cause. If people are sick from an infectious germ or "mysterious virus," we know that traumatic and chronic stress disrupt and weaken the effectiveness of the immune system to destroy invaders.

Traumatic and chronic stress are major factors in heart disease, cancer, and strokes. These three are the leading causes of death in the United States and account for 75 percent of all deaths. In 1900, cancer was the eighth leading cause of death. To realize how things have changed since 1900, compare the following information.

The ten leading causes of death in the United States:[2]

1900	*1981*
1. Pneumonia and influenza	1. Diseases of the heart
2. Tuberculosis	2. Cancer
3. Diarrhea and other intestinal diseases	3. Stroke
4. Diseases of the heart	4. Accident
5. Stroke	5. Lung disease including emphysema
6. Kidney diseases	6. Pneumonia and influenza
7. All accidents	7. Diabetes
8. Cancer	8. Chronic liver disease and cirrhosis
9. Senility	9. Atherosclerosis
10. Diphtheria	10. Suicide

We are paying an exorbitant price for living in our uptight, stress-filled world. We like to think we can live at our own hectic pace, abusing our bodies, eating junk food, drinking too much alcohol, and never missing a beat as we grab all the gusto we can. If we get sick or break down, we go to the physician for a shot, some medication or, if things are *really* bad, an operation, and in no time we will be better. In fact, some hard driving executives have already accepted the eventuality that in the near future they will need a triple heart bypass. It seems to me some kind of proof that they have given their all in the competitive drive for corporate success.

Seriously, can you afford to get sick and be hospitalized? A semiprivate room can cost from $250.00 to $500.00 a day, depending on where you live, and that's only the beginning. Have you heard about the woman suffering from a bad headache who went to the emergency room of a hospital? She was kept there for observation for two nights. Her bill was $1,226.55. Now that is expensive observation. Then there is the case of a man who went to a public hospital for a two-hour knee operation.

His bill for two and a half days was $12,046.00. At a Boston teaching hospital, a seventy-two-year-old man had a heart attack and arrived unconscious. After a week in a coma, he died. The bill—$12,578.00. In Los Angeles a person undergoing a common operation suffered brain death because of problems with the anesthesia. He was kept alive on life-support machines for six months. His bill was more than $1 million.[3] A woman was telling how her husband had died because of medical mistakes during heart bypass surgery. That was tragic enough, but she said the hospital keeps sending her bills for ongoing medical expenses—weeks after her husband's funeral.

The health care business is big business in the United States. If money could buy health, our nation would be the healthiest one on earth. In 1982 Americans spent $322 billion on health care, amounting to $1,365 for every man, woman, and child. The proportion of the gross national product going to health care exceeded 10 percent for the first time, going to 10.5 percent. In 1965 the health care costs were only 6 percent of the gross national product.[4]

The high costs of getting sick and of being hospitalized have created a revolution in the health care industry. Health Maintenance Organizations (HMO's) have grown rapidly to reduce medical costs. The small monthly fee and a token charge of $3 to $5 per visit to the doctor naturally appeal to consumers. In Arizona, for example, CIGNA is the largest HMO in the state. It employs around 250 doctors.

There are now rules and guidelines for how long a person can stay in a hospital for a certain medical problem. This approach does save money, but using a statistical average time can result in a person's leaving a hospital too soon after surgery.

Another new development is "surgicenters" where people can have needed surgery performed and go home the same day. These have proven to be very efficient and cost effective.

Staying out of hospitals or reducing the time spent in them

not only saves money but is good for your health. Hospitals can be hazardous to your health. Did you know that hospital-caused infections kill a minimum of twenty thousand people a year? The single biggest factor in causing these infections is the failure of doctors and nurses to wash their hands between patient examinations.[5] If I have to be a patient in a hospital, I am going to insist on watching the doctors and nurses wash their hands before I let them touch me.

I also believe patients become ill in hospitals because of the exhaustion of the interns and residents who are treating them. As the result of their inhuman work hours, often on duty for thirty-six hours at a stretch, working month after month without a day off, the doctors in training become ill from weakened immune systems and stress exhaustion. I once called our son, Danny, when he was interning in a hospital, and he was so sick with the flu he could barely talk. He was running a fever, too. I said that maybe he could get a few days off and catch up on his sleep. He replied that he could not take a day off because he was sick. I then asked what service he was on that month, and he replied, "Intensive Care."

The best way to save money on medical bills is simple: Don't get sick. There is an art to staying well. *Webster's New Collegiate Dictionary* defines *art* as "skill acquired by experience, study, or observation." We don't naturally have healthy habits nor have we learned how not to get sick. Have you ever asked a physician to teach you how *not* to get sick? The traditional medical model is a sickness model, not a health model. Doctors are trained in crisis medicine and how to help sick people get well.

The art of staying well will require the development of skills through practice and experience. It is an attitude, a philosophy, a personal decision, to be responsible for your life, your health, and your healing. It is a journey to a life-style of positive wellness. Prevention is an idea whose time has come.

The definition of health takes on a new perspective. The World Health Organization defines *health* as "a state of physical, mental and social well-being, and not merely the absence of disease or infirmity." I would add spiritual well-being to the definition.

In the new model of health, positive wellness, not just the absence of disease or infirmity, is the goal. Traditional medicine considers a person well if he has no symptoms and falls within the normal range in a series of diagnostic tests. This "well person," who may have recently experienced an increase in stress, may smoke heavily, consume too much alcohol, and eat 100 to 120 pounds of refined sugar a year. He is not examined for his eating habits or nutritional needs. This "well person" may not exercise and may be overweight and emotionally constipated. Actually, this person is not well but is in the process of "getting ready to get sick," according to the new definition of health.

The new revolution in health and healing will emphasize the interconnectedness and interrelationship of emotional, mental, spiritual, and environmental factors with physical health and healing. The physical body will no longer be viewed as a machine and reduced to smaller and smaller parts needing repairs. The whole person in his uniqueness will be emphasized. The great Canadian physician, Sir William Osler, said, "Ask not what kind of illness the patient has, ask what kind of patient has the illness."

The concept of wholeness is a very old concept in health. Socrates said over two thousand years ago, "As it is not proper to cure the eyes without the head, nor the head without the body, so neither is it proper to cure the body without the soul. There is no illness of the body apart from the mind."

Hippocrates believed, "In order to cure the human body, it is necessary to have a knowledge of the whole thing. The body is the physician of its own illness. A doctor is making a mistake if he believes that his is the sole responsibility for curing illness.

The physician is not the healer; the patient is. The job of the physician is to activate and use to the fullest the patient's healing mechanism, as well as to understand when and why the healing mechanism fails to work."

Arnold Hutschnecker, a medical doctor, writes, "But slowly, painfully, we are relearning in new ways the Hippocratic truth: If a part is ill, the whole is ill. Illness is more than a malfunctioning system or a diseased organ. Illness is the outer expression of a deep and possibly dangerous struggle going on within."[6]

It took me a long time to appreciate the profound truth in his statement. I found it harder than I realized to shift my thinking from the idea that illness is caused by a germ to the reality that it is an "outer expression of a deep and possibly dangerous struggle going on within."

An exciting phenomenon in our country is the journey to positive wellness that a vast segment of our population has begun. Millions of men and women have quit smoking and have demanded smoke-free work environments and nonsmoking areas in restaurants and other public places. Today, all smoking is forbidden on flights of two hours or less. Northwest has banned all smoking.

I never will forget a flight I was on some years ago, before there were prohibitions against smoking pipes or cigars and there were certainly no nonsmoking areas. Two seats ahead of me, a man pulled out a big cigar and lighted up. In the seat ahead of me was a tiny woman, I guess in her seventies. She asked the man if he would not smoke the cigar because cigar smoke made her very ill. He replied, "That's too bad, lady," and started to smoke the cigar. The elderly woman bent her head down, and I wondered if she was crying or looking for an airsick bag or both. What she was doing was searching in her purse. She soon found what she was looking for, got up from her seat, and walked to the aisle where the cigar smoker was puffing away. She then took her scissors and cut off the cigar, which fell into the man's lap. Every person in that section of the plane applauded. The woman never said a word. She returned to her seat and put her scissors back into her purse. Now that was a touch of class.

Many Americans have recognized the value of exercise and are doing something about it. In 1961, the Gallup Polls indicated that approximately 24 percent of adults in the United States exercised regularly. That figure increased to 47 percent by 1977, and recent trends indicate an ever-greater rise in the future. There is no simple explanation for this trend that involves nearly 100 million people. And it was characterized by George Gallup as one of the most dramatic changes in life-style he has ever measured in his public polls.

A few years ago, if you saw someone running in your neighborhood, you immediately thought he was a burglar. But now you know, with all the jogging that is taking place, he is just someone staying healthy.

Attitudes toward food are also changing. People are seeking a life-style of better nutrition, cutting back on animal fat, refined sugar, alcohol, and caffeine. Just look at the number of television commercials promoting healthy food and drinks. Health food stores are everywhere. Health is in, far more than at any other time in our country's history. What is so remarkable is that these behavioral changes in regard to positive wellness came about without a government program or the American Medical Association sponsoring or promoting them. In fact, the average consumer probably has read more about nutrition and health than the average physician.

American corporations have become vitally interested in the health of their employees and are developing positive wellness programs at a record rate. There are very real economic reasons for this concern. In 1981, premature deaths cost industry $25 billion, and lost workdays that year cost $132 billion. Just replacing victims of heart attacks cost industry $700 million in 1981.

Kenneth R. Pelletier cites these examples of costs that are forcing business and industry to confront issues of health and disease prevention.

1. A recent study indicated that smoking cost employers $27.5 billion with $8.2 billion in direct medical costs and $19.3 billion in indirect costs such as absenteeism.
2. For alcohol abuse alone, the total costs were $44.2 billion. Alcoholic employees experience twice the rate of absenteeism.
3. General Motors spent more money, $82.5 million per year, on health insurance and disabilities than on steel from U.S. Steel, one of its principal suppliers.
4. Similarly, Ford Motor Company estimates health care costs per employee at $3,350 per year and $290 per automobile the year of 1980.
5. In 1980 the National Institute for Occupational Safety and Health estimated the cost of "executive stress" alone at $10 billion to $20 billion in the United States. That figure covers only the clearly measurable items as workdays lost, hospitalization, outpatient care and mortality.[7]

I never realized the extent of the effect of employees' sickness on corporate profits and consumer prices for the items produced by industry. The growing corporate interest in employee health was confirmed in a 1985 survey by the U.S. Department of Health and Human Services. According to the survey results, almost two-thirds of American work force sites with fifty or more employees have at least one health promotion activity.

Smoking cessation topped the list of corporate-sponsored health activities, which also included the following:

- health risk assessment
- back care
- stress management
- exercise and fitness
- off-the-job accident prevention
- nutrition education
- high blood pressure control
- weight control

There is also a very real concern for accident prevention on the job as well as for toxic health hazards in the job environment.

The key to successful corporate programs in positive wellness is found in the joint participation of management and employees to reach that goal. Personal responsibility for staying well is stressed. In fact, some companies have eliminated sick leave pay and reward employees financially for being well. Healthy people are happier and are more productive. If the management shows concern for and commitment to the health of employees, and if the employees are in on the planning and working of the program, the company will have not only well employees, which will save millions of dollars each year, but loyal and motivated workers. Profits will increase as a natural by-product of this type of participating, caring management.

I think it's time to tell you about myself. Ordained a Lutheran pastor in 1954, I was called to develop a home mission congregation in Canoga Park, California. As a pastor I did a lot of counseling, and so I took courses in clinical psychology to help me grow as a counselor. In 1957 I read Hans Selye's *The Stress of Life,* which sparked an ongoing interest in learning more about the acute and chronic stress in people's lives. In 1965 I decided to attend Arizona State University to begin work on a doctorate in counseling psychology. I interned for twenty hours a week on the children's psychiatric unit of the Arizona State Hospital. I finished my doctorate in June 1967.

In December 1965, Omer K. Reed, D.D.S., asked me to teach a course in human communications to a group of dentists. Dental professionals are quite committed to continuing education, and Dr. Reed was instrumental in getting me involved in lecturing for the American Society for Preventive Dentistry and in serving on its board of directors for many years. It was through my association with dentistry that I became aware of the important role nutrition plays in promoting health and of the role stress and emotional conflicts play in the chronic pain of the temporomandibular joint syndrome.

In 1975 I temporarily closed down my private clinical psychology practice so that I could devote the next three years to self-directed study into the interaction of the emotions, the mind, the spirit, the body, nutrition, relationships, and environment in health and healing. It was a time of exciting growth for me. What I learned I use now in my clinical practice. I realized anew that my most valuable possession is my health. Since I am not going to get out of this thing alive, I've decided to live a full, healthy life with a sense of humor and love until the day I die. I have decided that I want to die healthy.

My hope is that you learn something about the art of staying well and that you make a commitment to start the journey into positive wellness.

NOTES

1. James McKeever, "Aids: The Plague That Knows No Boundaries," *End-Time News Digest* (published by Omega Ministries, Medford, Oreg.), July 1987.
2. Christine Russell, "Holding the Line on Disease," *The Arizona Republic,* April 24, 1987.

3. "Soaring Hospital Costs," *U.S. News & World Report,* August 22, 1983.

4. "Health," *The Arizona Republic,* July 7, 1983.

5. Philip J. Hilts, "Catching Your Death in Hospitals," *The Arizona Republic,* April 27, 1983.

6. Arnold A. Hutschnecker, *The Will to Live* (New York: Cornerstone Library, 1974).

7. Kenneth R. Pelletier, *Healthy People in Unhealthy Places* (New York: Delacorte Press/Seymour Lawrence, 1984).

CHAPTER TWO

THE ANATOMY OF STRESS

It's tune-up time for a symphony orchestra before a major performance. Many of the musicians are exhibiting signs of nervous anticipation of the concert. Mouths are dry, palms are moist, and some musicians, struggling with lower bowel nervousness, make repeated trips to the rest room. Now there is a moment of silence as all tuning stops and the spotlight focuses on the conductor who strides toward the podium amidst the applause of the audience in the concert hall.

The musicians rivet their eyes on the conductor as he taps the music stand and raises his baton. With the downstroke, the music begins. As the first notes are played, the nervousness vanishes; a surge of energy rushes through the musicians. All the hours of practice are worth the effort as the sound of the orchestra is alive with harmonious vibrations. The conductor's face is glowing with pride and satisfaction. It is as if each musician is reaching deep down inside for that little extra expression of his or her gift of music.

The music of the symphony orchestra is more than just a mechanical performance of the right notes being played in time. There is transcendence in the music. The audience is swept away with the force of the experience as the orchestra climbs to the dramatic climax of Tchaikovsky's *1812 Overture,* the exhilarating crescendo with cymbals clashing, kettledrums pounding, finally ending with the startling explosion of the cannon.

As the sounds fade, the crowd is automatically on its feet, applauding and shouting, "Bravo! Bravo!" as the conductor and the musicians take several well-deserved bows.

It has been a "peak experience" for each participant, the conductor, the orchestra, and the crowd. The music hall empties with the walls still vibrating from the energy released through the music.

Musicians drift off into the night with most of them going to their favorite restaurant for a late night dinner to celebrate and to gradually come down from the high of the adrenaline flowing through their bloodstreams. Finally, a good sense of tiredness informs them that it is time for sleep, which restores inner harmony and balance within their bodies. This is the anatomy of *acute stress.*

For the sake of illustration, let's say that instead of the musicians going home after the performance, they have to remain in the music hall for a long practice session, especially the last part of the *1812 Overture.* They repeat that piece of music hour after hour through the night with just a few hours off for rest and then go back to work. Hour after hour, day after day, week after week, until all the people in the orchestra collapse.

What section would collapse first? The string section? The percussion section? How long would the oboe and bassoon players be able to maintain their "pucker power"?

Playing that crescendo over and over, with cymbals clashing, kettledrums pounding, and cannon booming, would unleash a bundle of nervous symptoms. Nerves and muscles would start twitching, heads would pound, tempers would flare, and fights would break out. Even a few hours off for sleep would not help because the heart would continue to pound and blood pressure would throb in the ears from the constant flow of adrenaline that refuses to shut down. The music has been reduced to a cacophony of discordant sound.

In every area of the musicians' bodies are very painful muscle spasms. Blood pressures are dangerously high. Finally, of the musicians who are left, there is total collapse into depression, apathy, and exhaustion. Thus, a fine symphony orchestra is destroyed. This is the anatomy of *chronic stress*.

The years pass. The musicians gather for a reunion. As each arrives, it is soon evident that this once fine symphony orchestra is now a health disaster group. Twisted fingers from arthritis mean that some will never play another note of music. There are the ones with bleeding ulcers, colitis, chronic migraines, high blood pressure—and these are the healthier ones. Several of the group are dead from coronaries, cancer, strokes, and suicide. Still others are recovering from heart bypass surgery, from chemotherapy for cancer, and from partial paralysis following strokes. There are also the musicians who have serious kidney diseases, rheumatoid arthritis, multiple sclerosis, and lupus. Even the "healthier" ones are addicted to drugs like cocaine, heroin, and alcohol.

One of the kettledrummers and two cymbal players were mysteriously murdered, but no one was ever arrested for the crimes. Many in the orchestra have a good idea who the murderer is but will never tell.

Rumors abound that the conductor will not show for the reunion, but finally, there he is, being led into the room by a friend. He is blind and deaf.

In this illustration I have tried to show the difference between the normal stress response and the destructiveness of chronic stress.

Stress stimulates mental, emotional, hormonal, and neurophysiological responses that cause a person to adapt to its challenge. Hans Selye was the pioneer researcher in stress until his death in 1982. He taught that the changes brought about by the challenge to a person are the body's adaptive reaction, which he called the general adaptive syndrome. The general adaptive syndrome consists of three stages: (1) the alarm reaction; (2) adaptation or resistance; and (3) exhaustion and distress.

In the first stage the alarm reaction sets off an automatic response in the body to meet the challenge. The body is ready for what has been called the "fight or flight" response. It is a call to arms within the body. The second stage occurs when all the adaptive energies and hormones of the stress response are utilized to adapt to the challenge and resist it. If the person meets the challenge and then is able to return to normal functioning, the inner balance of the body chemistry is restored to a normal balance (or homeostasis). Remember how the members of the symphony orchestra met the challenge and then went out to dinner to relax and come down off their adrenaline high. By morning, the inner balance was restored. The stress response brought out the best in the musicians, so it was a very helpful response.

An athletic coach knows that the key to having his team ready for a game is to have the positive response peak during the beginning of the game. If a team peaks with the stress response too soon, the team will be "flat," and probably nothing will help fire the stress response during the game.

Under chronic stress, the body's adaptive energy is depleted, and an imbalance within the body chemistry sends out hormones. Because of the body's constant state of "red alert," there will be exhaustion, physical collapse, and even death. This third stage of the general adaptive syndrome was illustrated by the destruction of the musicians in the never-ending rehearsals of the *1812 Overture*.

In one of his experiments Selye exposed rats to such extreme stressors as cold, forced muscular exercise, bone fracture, and so on. These stress-producing agents were of constant intensity, and they made demands for long periods of time. No matter what type of damage was inflicted on the rats, the following three symptoms were produced:

1. The adrenal cortex became enlarged and revealed adrenal exhaustion.
2. The thymus, spleen, lymph nodes, and all other lymphatic structures showed extreme atrophy. In other words, the immune system was shriveled up and useless.
3. Deep bleeding ulcers appeared in the stomach and duodenum.

The result of chronic stress and exhaustion of the adaptive energy in the rats led to death.[1] (Someday mankind should build a monument to the white rat in honor of the many white rats who have given their lives to help scientists deal with human illnesses.)

The stimulus that triggers the stress response begins with a little gland in the midpoint of the brain called the hypothalamus. The hypothalamus sends a message to the pituitary gland, which release chemical messengers to the rest of the endocrine system, including the thyroid and adrenal glands. The chain reaction of the stress response results in the following things happening within a person to adapt to and resist the challenge.

The adrenal glands release the hormones for fight or flight. You are familiar with the rush of energy from the adrenal glands when you are driving a car and suddenly you see a child chasing a ball dart out in front of your car. You slam on the brakes in time to avoid a tragic accident. Your heart pounds faster. Your blood pressure rises because the blood vessels constrict, almost closing the blood vessels just under the skin, giving your hands that cold, clammy effect. Your facial muscles contract, expressing strong emotion. Nostrils and throat passages are wide open. Moisture in your mouth decreases while perspiration increases. The flow of blood goes to the large muscles to bring more oxygen and energy for action. The stomach and intestines halt the digestive process. The flow of blood to the muscles controlling the bladder and bowels decreases.

The ancient Chinese must have known about this decrease in saliva, for they used this reaction as an old-fashioned lie detector test. They put rice in the mouth of suspects in a crime and, on command, told the suspects to swallow the rice. The guilty ones, who were experiencing stress, could not swallow the rice because it was "dry rice."

The anticipation of an event can start the stress response in the body. When I was playing football in high school, I would be afflicted with diarrhea in anticipation of the kickoff. One of my fellow players was nicknamed W. W. Wilmoth, for "Wee Wee" Wilmoth, because the anticipatory response of stress caused a problem of bladder control. I was the fullback, and W. W. was the quarterback. Together we would be in the locker room up to the last minute. As soon as the kickoff took place, though, everything was all right.

Inside the body during the stress response, the liver is releasing stored energy into the bloodstream in the form of glucose and cholesterol. The adrenals also release fat into the blood for energy.

The spleen releases more red corpuscles to enable the blood to clot more quickly, and the bone marrow produces more white corpuscles to strengthen the immune system. To help fight infections, the adrenals release inflammatory hormones, and the resulting inflammation will actually wall off invading microbes and destroy them.

Kidneys are essential organs in handling stress. Through their elimination function, the kidneys regulate the chemical composition and water content of the blood and tissues to maintain the body's inner balance. They also get rid of toxic substances.

What I've provided here is a very simplified description of the normal stress response, but you can readily see how pervasive are the effects on the body.

Living with chronic stress is different from dealing with acute stress. Having chronic stress means that your body is getting ready to get sick. The area of weakness or predisposition in your body will be the first area to be affected by chronic stress.

Here is a list of warning signals of chronic stress.

1. Exhaustion and lack of energy or interest in anything, even sex, are the norms, not the exceptions.
2. You experience mental fatigue to the degree you find it more and more difficult to concentrate and remember things. Your mind is flooded with disconnected thoughts.
3. You have difficulty sleeping. Perhaps you wake up at 2:00 or 3:00 A.M. and are not able to get back to sleep because you feel so wired and your heart is pounding. Even if you do sleep through the night, you don't feel rested when you wake up. Nightmares about death or tragedy may haunt you. Upon awakening, your fists are clenched, and your jaw muscles are tense from grinding your teeth.
4. You lack emotional control. You cry easily, blow up easily, and feel irritable. You would like to run away and hide and have a pity party. You feel you just can't go on because you are so depressed and nothing interests you.
5. You are easily startled by small sounds. In fact, you are anxious most of the time.

6. Your voice becomes high pitched, and you talk in machine-gun spurts.
7. You suffer from eating disorders—ranging from loss of appetite to eating everything in sight. Of course your digestive tract is a mess. You go from diarrhea to constipation in one day.
8. You are frequently subject to the pain of headaches, neckaches, backaches, or sciatica.

So, how do you try to combat chronic stress? Usually in the wrong way. If you smoke, you smoke more than ever in an effort to obtain extra energy from the nicotine.

You either stop eating or eat all the wrong foods, such as junk foods.

You try to get more energy by drinking more coffee or soft drinks.

You can't sleep, so you begin to take pills to get you to sleep, or drink too much alcohol, or both. Then you take pep pills in the morning to get going.

You might take up exercising because you are so exhausted, but after a little exercise, you are more exhausted than ever since you just burned up what little energy you had left.

You deny that you need a vacation for two weeks just to rest and you use the excuse that you are too far behind at work, or you are so addicted to your adrenaline habit that you find it impossible to slow down long enough to go through withdrawal.

By this time, you are ready to get sick because your immune system is weakened by chronic stress. You could have a coronary, a stroke, or a life-crippling or life-threatening disease.

In the nineteenth century Louis Pasteur discovered the microbe and the germ theory of disease. This theory proposed that illness or disease is caused by one or more germs invading the body and causing the person to become ill. Thus, for years the approach of modern medicine has been to find a drug to kill the germs. A pill for every ill became the goal. Unfortunately, even germs have adaptive mechanisms. "Virtually all disease organisms are becoming more and more resistant to drugs. If we continue to use antibiotics freely," said Walter Gilbert, a Nobel laureate in biochemistry, "there may be a time down the road when 80 to 90 percent of infections will be resistant to all known antibiotics. The common dose of penicillin required to treat an infection today is 50 times the size of the dose used to treat the same infection 30 years ago."[2]

Claude Bernard, a French physiologist and a contemporary of Louis Pasteur, disagreed with Pasteur's different views of why people became ill. Bernard believed that illnesses hover constantly above us, their seeds blown by the wind, but they do not set in the terrain unless the terrain is ready to receive them. For Bernard, the terrain was the human body, a collection of cells and systems that are constantly shifting, altering and adjusting to pressures from within the person and from without. If the internal conditions were fertile enough for the germs to flourish, then that person was ready to succumb to some disease. If the internal environment of the body was in a proper balance and the immune system working at maximum capacity, germs would not take root. It has been said that when Pasteur was on his death bed, he said, "Bernard was right. The microbe is nothing, the terrain is everything."

How to live with stress successfully is to realize the truth of Selye's key belief that "it's not the amount of stress you have; it's how you respond to it." Stress is definitely linked to heart disease, strokes, cancer, arthritis, ulcers, kidney disease, and other diseases. But stress isn't the cause of such diseases, Selye insisted; "[the cause is] the reaction to stress when the reaction is 'dis-stress.'"

Selye stated that "adaptability is probably the most distinctive characteristic of life." When he was challenged to adapt to one of the most malignant cancers known, he said,

> I was sure I was going to die. So I said to myself, "All right, this is about the very worst thing that could happen to you, but there are two ways you can handle that. Either you can go around feeling like a miserable candidate on death row and whimper away a year, or else you can try to squeeze as much from life now as you can."'
>
> I chose the latter because I'm a fighter and cancer provided me with the biggest challenge of my life. I took it as a natural experiment that pushed me to the ultimate test of whether I was right or wrong. Then a strange thing happened. A year went by. Then two. Then three—and look what happened. It turned out I was that fortunate exception.[3]

Selye believed that change produced the stress response and it did not matter whether or not it was pleasant. What matters is the intensity of the adaptation to the change.

For some people, security is in their environment, their hometown, relatives, friends, and the external continuity of their lives. Reaction to change, such as moving thousands of miles away from a small hometown to a large metropolitan city, would create a powerful stress response for those persons.

For the person whose security is within himself and who believes that no matter what changes come along, he will adapt and land on his feet, a move to a new city would not be as stressful or threatening to his emotional security.

Thomas Holmes and Richard Rahe, psychiatrists at the University of Washington, have devised a scale and assigned point values to changes that affect us. The scale dramatically focuses on how much change a person can take within one year of life. When the point values for the various changes occurring in one year add up to 300, a person is at a critical point.

Of the people studied, 80 percent who exceeded 300

points became seriously depressed, had heart attacks, or suffered from other serious illness. Now, if persons score over 300 points, it doesn't mean they have to suffer from any of those health problems because 20 percent of those in the study did not get sick or die. The difference for that group had to be in the way they reacted to changes and how they perceived changes. I wish Holmes and Rahe had extensively studied the secrets of health for the 20 percent.

Life Change	Points
Death of spouse	100
Divorce	73
Marital separation	65
Jail term	63
Death of close family member	63
Personal injury or illness	53
Marriage	50
Fired from job	47
Marital reconciliation	45
Retirement	45
Change in health of family member	44
Pregnancy	40
Sex difficulties	39
Gain of new family member	39
Change in financial status	38
Death of close friend	37
Change to different kind of work	36
Change in number of arguments with spouse	35
Foreclosure of mortgage or loan	30
Change in work responsibilities	29
Son or daughter leaving home	29

Trouble with in-laws	29
Outstanding personal achievement	28
Wife beginning or stopping work	26
Beginning or ending school	26
Revision of personal habits	24
Trouble with boss	23
Change in residence	20
Change in schools	20
Vacation	13
Minor violations of law	11

The Greek philosopher Epictetus wrote, "Man is not disturbed by things, but by his opinion about things."[4] I would like you to examine your daily life for the things that trigger the stress response in you or get you uptight. Make a list of them, and check the things that you cannot change in your life. For the things that you can change, develop a plan of action. For the things that you cannot change, remember you can alter your reaction to them. After you have written down the things that get you uptight, you may be surprised to find that most of those things are not things or events at all, but people. And it is possible, after all, to control your emotional reactions to those people. The emotions are yours, not the other way around.

In *The Art of Hanging Loose in an Uptight World,* I wrote,

How often are you in charge of what is happening to you? Are you guilty of waiting for someone's action to dictate your frame of mind? Is your life pattern that of waiting for someone else to make you feel good or important? And then, do you feel that you've been ignored or that no one cares? In short, do you feel convinced that others are responsible for the way you feel?

I've got a bulletin: nobody makes you feel any way you don't want to feel.[5]

As you examine your list of things and people that make you uptight, examine the areas where you are able to exert control over what happens to you daily. The less control you have over your life, the more stress you experience within and the more you live a life of frustration. Frustration is that trapped feeling of having little or no control over the important events in your life.

Innumerable articles, books, and seminars have focused on executive stress, but the truth is that executives have a distinct advantage over their employees because they have more control over their jobs. From my experience, I have found that most high-level executives thrive on stress and actively seek it. It motivates and exhilarates them. They are basically high-risk people. Stressful things to them would be living without challenge and having nothing to look forward to the next day. Too little stimulation of the stress response would be hazardous to their health.

The most stressful jobs are those in which persons have the least control over their lives, such as secretaries, laborers, middle managers, and nurses. There is a serious shortage of nurses in our country because they are leaving their profession due to too much stress and low financial rewards not commensurate with the responsibility of their work. On the counter of a nurses' station in a hospital I saw this sign: "If you are looking for someone with a little authority around here, I have as little authority as anyone here." A nurse is responsible for the patients assigned for care, responsible to the physicians of the patients, to the nursing supervisor, and to the hospital administration, which is exerting more pressure on the nursing staff by demanding better care for the patients and more time-consuming paperwork while at the same time cutting administrative expenses by hiring fewer nurses. An added conflict arises from differences among the people who oversee the nurses, with the nurses caught in the middle.

The work itself is not the cause of destructive stress, but the feeling that management doesn't care what is happening to the employees or doesn't even know why the employees are unhappy. Top management in industry basically has not developed the interest or skill in listening to employees. One of the classic indications of a breakdown in communications systems in a business is "memo mania"—stacks of unnecessary memos that no one reads or cares about. Poor communications systems lead to an atmosphere of high fear and low trust among employees, which results in apathy, feelings of powerlessness, and frustration. This is a major source of chronic stress in industry.

Stress management techniques have been developed to help people cope with the problem of being uptight and stressful. Incorporating these techniques into one's daily life is effective in counteracting chronic stress. Some of these techniques are listed below.

1. Use a relaxation technique, such as visualization of peaceful scenes, to develop the relaxation response, the opposite of the fight-flight response.
2. Exercise to burn up excess adrenaline in the bloodstream. Safest exercises include walking, swimming, and riding an exercycle. Exercise is not beneficial when a person is in a chronic stage of stress exhaustion.
3. Learn how to say no to the demands that disturb your inner peace, and then don't feel guilty.
4. Learn how to have fun, but be careful not to make "fun" another form of competitive work.
5. Forgive those who have hurt you and forgive yourself. No one is perfect. Look what happened to the only person who was perfect—Jesus.
6. Simplify your life.

7. Manage your finances so you won't always be living from paycheck to paycheck. Reduce your indebtedness. Financial problems bring out the worst in the best of us, especially in marriage.
8. Develop healthy, nutritious eating habits.
9. Give yourself permission to develop your own unique interests and live in the here and now. Live with more joy, peace, and love in your life.

Stress reduction techniques are designed primarily to help you adapt and cope with symptoms of stress. The major solution to living with stress successfully is learning the art of staying well through a life-style of positive wellness.

NOTES

1. Hans Selye, "Stress: The Basis of Illness" in *Inner Balance*, ed. Elliot M. Goldway (Englewood Cliffs, N.J.: Prentice-Hall, 1979).
2. Christine Russell, "Holding the Line on Disease," *The Arizona Republic*, April 24, 1983.
3. Hans Selye, "It's Not the Amount of Stress You Have. It's How You Respond to It," *Executive Health* 19 (February 1983).
4. T. H. Holmes and R. H. Rahe, "Schedule of Recent Experience [SRE]," Department of Psychiatry, University of Washington School of Medicine, 1967.
5. Ken Olson, *The Art of Hanging Loose in an Uptight World* (New York: Fawcett, 1975; Phoenix: O'Sullivan Woodside, 1974).

CHAPTER THREE

THE HEALING WARRIORS WITHIN

O ne of the most harmful effects of chronic stress is the damage it does to the immune system. In the immune system are the powerful healing warriors that produce trillions of kinds of antibodies to fight diseases. This complex system must respond quickly to all external challenges and be incredibly precise in first recognizing the type of threat and then producing the right antibodies needed to kill foreign and abnormal cells attempting to destroy the body's healthy cells.

As important as the immune system is to our health and healing, it had been virtually ignored by the scientific medical community until the past few years. In fact, before 1960, scientists did not see the significance of the thymus gland in regard to the immune system. It was viewed as a useless vestige, like the appendix, with no vital function. During chest surgery, a surgeon would often remove the thymus, only to wonder why the patient died shortly thereafter of some infection or disease.

The failure of traditional methods of treating cancer with chemotherapy, radiation, and surgery has caused researchers to investigate the immune system and ways to enhance its power to fight cancer. So instead of destroying or severely damaging them with radiation therapy and chemotherapy, scientists are treating the healing warriors of the immune system with great respect.

The horror of AIDS (Acquired Immune Deficiency Syndrome) has created a worldwide demand for research concerning the workings of the immune system in order to find a cure for the virus that attacks the system by killing helper T cells and macrophages, thus preventing the body from producing antibodies and destroying invading organisms. AIDS victims eventually die from infections because the immune system fails to fight them off; therefore, AIDS is classified as an immunodeficiency disease. Susumu Tonegawa, a Japanese researcher working in the United States, won the Nobel Prize in medicine in Stockholm, Sweden, on October 12, 1987, for discovering how the body makes millions of kinds of antibodies to fight disease. No longer can the field of immunology say, like Rodney Dangerfield, "I get no respect."

Our immune system is composed of billions of white blood cells that travel through the thymus, the lymphatic system, the bloodstream, and the spleen. I would like to use a simple way of describing how the healing warriors of this system function.

From the thymus gland come the helper T cells, the killer T cells, and the suppressor T cells. The helper T cells spot trouble, turn on the immune system, and help organize B cells and killer T cells. The killer T cells are born killers of viruses, germs, cancerous cells, and so on. Suppressor T cells are the watchmen of the immune system serving the function of preventing killer T cells and B cells from getting trigger happy, turning on healthy cells in the body, and destroying them as well as germs. The suppressor T cells turn off the immune system response.

The B cells come from the bone marrow and have an

amazing ability to manufacture antibodies or poison to kill invading germs and then to forever remember the profiles of those germs. Other powerful warriors are the macrophages from the bone marrow, which are scavenger cells that act like a "Pac-Man" in consuming dead bacteria and destroying other invading organisms.

The battle can be pictured in this way. One day helper T cells are cruising through the bloodstream when they spot a group of strangers in the blood, so they go up to the strangers and say, "You're new in town, aren't you?"

"Yeah, so what?" one of the strangers replies.

"Well, you look like you are up to no good in here," says a helper T cell. "What are your names?"

"Just call me 'Mysterious Virus.' Now what are you going to do about it?"

He replies, "I've brought a whole gang with me. You'll be sorry you came here." And with a loud voice he yells, "Help!" Instantly the Mysterious Virus gang is surrounded by killer T cells who begin to do their thing—killing. B cells come to their assistance, put into their computers the chemical makeup of the Mysterious Viruses, and soon produce a specific antibody, a poison to kill the strangers. They immediately store this information in their memory bank just in case the Mysterious Viruses ever come around again. Next time there will be no mystery, and death to the intruders will soon follow.

The macrophages destroy and devour the remains of the Mysterious Viruses and thus eliminate the waste. Meanwhile the suppressor T cells are vigilantly watching to make sure the killer T cells and the B cells don't get carried away in the frenzy of battle and begin to attack healthy, normal cells when the battle is won. The suppressor T cells turn off the immune system, and all is peaceful and quiet again. Ironically, the person may not even know that a great battle against a virus was fought and won by the healing warriors within. The only hint of trouble may have been a slight fever for a while.

The immune system has to maintain a delicate balance because any imbalance can be hazardous to a person's health. If there are too few helper T cells, the immune system will react sluggishly to germs or viruses. If there are too few suppressor T cells to regulate the activity of the killer T cells and the B cells, the immune system can malfunction; the killer T cells and B cells can attack healthy cells and tissue in the body, resulting in autoimmune diseases such as powerful allergic reactions, rheumatoid arthritis, lupus, multiple sclerosis, or myasthenia gravis.

When the immune system is in balance, the killer T cells just cruise through the bloodstream searching for any harmful agents. Often they rest in the spleen and lymph nodes, awaiting their call to action. The killer T cells cause rejection of organ transplants, such as a kidney or heart. The killer T cells identify the transplanted organ as a foreign invader and declare war on it to destroy it. To prevent rejection of the transplanted organ, the person is given powerful drugs to suppress the immune response of rejection. However, when the immune system is suppressed, it is also weakened in fighting off other infections or cancer cells.

One of the things that astounds me is how a killer T cell knows when a good, healthy cell has become a dangerous, mutinous cancer cell. The human brain, amazing and wonderful as it is, wouldn't recognize a mutinous cancer cell if it saw it, yet the healing warriors of the immune system do it all the time. Our bodies produce cancer cells innumerable times. Most of us have probably had cancer at one time or another, but we have not been aware of it since the healing warriors have been so effective in protecting us.

Cancer appears when the immune system is weakened,

inhibited, or suppressed. Following are some of the ways the immune system is weakened and made less effective in the battle against viruses, bacteria, cancer, or fungi.

In 1986 when there was a nuclear disaster at the Chernobyl Nuclear Power Plant in the Soviet Union, the high levels of radiation destroyed immune systems of exposed workers and, as a result, killed them.

The three basic medical weapons in the war against cancer are radiation, chemotherapy, and surgery. Radiation and chemotherapy kill the cancer cells as well as healthy cells. One of the greatest side effects of both chemotherapy and radiation is the destruction of bone marrow and the B cells of the immune system. The fields of immunology and cancer research are now seeking ways to strengthen the immune response instead of weakening it by radiation and chemotherapy. "The side effects of radiotherapy and chemotherapy," says Drs. Remington and Krahebukl of the Palo Alto Medical Research Foundation and Stanford Medical School, "can seriously restrict the patient's ability to mount an immune response. We bomb our own troops so to speak. Let's look at a viable alternative way."[1]

Chemotherapy and radiation therapy can destroy existing cancer cells, but the immune system is so weakened and suppressed that it most likely would fail to meet the challenge of new cancer cells developing later on. The person's healing warriors would no longer be powerful enough to defeat the cancer cells, so the result would be death.

Now, remember that the B cells of the immune system use a computerlike memory bank to recognize and diagnose the makeup of a germ or cancerous cell. After having once recorded this information, the B cells will never forget it. Even more amazing is the ability to manufacture the proper antibodies and release them to circulate in the blood where they can reach and attack an intruding foe within five seconds.

If cancer cells develop into a tumor, then the type of cancer is diagnosed, stored in the memory bank of the B cell, and the specific antibody needed to kill this type of cancer is produced. The antibody goes directly to the tumor and locks on to the cancer cells.

Medical science is using this information by taking the antibodies produced in the immune system for a particular form of cancer, isolating the antibody, and making exact replicas or clones of it in unlimited quantities. The replicas are injected into the person with that type of cancer, and the clone antibodies not only fight and destroy the cancer cells, but also stimulate the whole immune system to produce more healing warriors.

How to stimulate the body's immune system so the healing warriors can multiply and attack with greater power against diseases like cancer is now a major focus of research. In the movie *Joey*, which is the story of Heisman Trophy winner John Cappelletti and his younger brother Joey's fight against leukemia, the ravages of leukemia and the chemotherapy had so weakened and suppressed Joey's immune system that when he contracted chicken pox, he almost died.

His body's last line of defense was to go into a coma. While he was in a coma, fighting for his life against chicken pox, his physician commented that Joey's leukemia was in remission. The immune system is like a battered boxer at times. When it received the challenge of Joey's chicken pox, it figuratively got up off the canvas to fight again. The invading germs of chicken pox stimulated the immune system's healing warriors to multiply and destroy any foreigner in the body that didn't belong there, including leukemia.

Next, I'll give you a glimpse of some of the exciting research being done on the immune system. Please remember, though, that this is an exploding area of knowledge. Much of this report will soon be out of date.

In 1978, it was reported that Dr. Martin F. McKneally,

along with a group of colleagues at Albany Medical College, used a new strategy of stimulating the immune system to combat lung cancer. After surgery for lung cancer, twenty-five patients were administered a preparation of live, but weakened, tuberculosis organisms designed to stimulate the patient's immune systems. During the next twelve months, not one patient died, but during the same period, nine of twenty-five other patients not receiving the tuberculosis organisms died.[2]

During the 1970s, we heard of promising new therapies from the immune system's lymphokines that regulate the immune system. Interferon became the new hope for finding a cure for cancer. The three types of interferon are alpha, beta, and gamma. Interferon is produced by killer T cells and triggers a mechanism within each cell that keeps viruses and bacteria from multiplying. It was hoped that interferon would be helpful in the treatment of cancer because it also changes the rate at which cells reproduce, and cancer cells are known for their wild rate of reproduction. Interferon was also believed to stimulate the production of B cells and macrophages.

At first scientists tried to extract interferon from the blood, but it was too difficult and too expensive. It cost $50,000 a gram! Now, thanks to genetic engineering, scientists can take the gene for interferon from a human cell, put it into a common germ that grows in a vat of yeast, and thus make the protein warriors of interferon in potentially limitless quantities.

Alpha interferon has been effective in fighting two types of leukemia and a cancer of the lymphatic system.

Gamma interferon appears to stimulate the immune response to stop and kill solid cancerous tumors, chronic leukemia, kidney cancer, and Kaposi's hemorrhage sarcoma, the cancer to which AIDS victims are particularly susceptible.[3] Gamma interferon is not poisonous to healthy cells as chemotherapy drugs are; it seems to be able to discriminate between tumors and normal tissue.

Have you ever heard of the "Luke Brothers" of the immune system? The scientific name for "Big Luke 1" is inter-leukin 1, a relative of gamma interferon. Both are products of the immune system, and both are powerful regulators of in-flammation and tissue destruction. As I have said earlier, when there are not enough suppressor T cells in the immune system, the powerful killer T cells can attack healthy cells, causing autoimmune diseases like rheumatoid arthritis. Now scientists are researching ways to inhibit the production of interleukin 1 and gamma interferon to prohibit the inflammatory effects of rheumatoid arthritis.[4] "Big Luke 2," or interleukin 2, has promising results in treating advanced skin cancer and kidney cancers. Dr. Jordan Gutterman of the Anderson Hospital and Tumor Institute believes there appears to be a "tremendous synergy" between alpha interferon and interleukin 2 in attack-ing cancer cells. Although interleukin 2 works to make the killer cells more potent, they have to recognize something unique on the surface of the cancer cell in order to kill it. That something is called an antigen, and interferon seems to make it more visible to the killer cells.[5]

The way to describe an antigen is to say that cancer cells release a chemical signal, like a chemical radar signal, which sounds the trumpet call to the killer cells to attack and "punch out" and destroy the cancer cells. A highly specific chemical warfare is being waged in the body. If the immune system is weakened and suppressed, then cancerous cells can escape de-tection and lodge in the body and begin to mutiply. Cancer cells are also very diabolic in that often the antigen, the radar signal, is covered by a fibrin coat that hides the antigen so the immune system is not activated to attack the cancer cell. That is why it is important for interleukin 2 to make the antigen more visible on the cancer cell in order to kill it. Scientists are also exploring chemicals that will strip off the cocoonlike covering over the cancer cell and its antigen.

New research and treatment are being done with bone

marrow transplants in fighting leukemia and treating congential immunodeficiency diseases in which children die from infections because they are unable to produce lymphocytes. The treatment involves taking bone marrow cells from a close relative of the patient and removing the normal cells that would attack the new bone marrow cells as foreign cells. Then these normal transplanted cells can repopulate a child's deficient immune system and correct the problem, thus saving the child's life.

One fascinating work in developing powerful healing warriors of the immune system is called hybridoma. This hybrid is perhaps one of the most bizarre creatures ever created. It is made up of a B cell, which produces antibodies, and a white cancer cell called myeloma. When these two cells are fused, the result is a hybrid that produces antibodies and lives forever. The hybrid can be made to produce antibodies to kill any virus, germ, or cancer. These are called monoclonal antibodies because they are specific, unique to one particular germ or cancer.[6]

As we grow older, we suffer not from "tired blood," but from a tired, run-down immune system that does not produce enough interleukin 1 to stimulate the production of more T cells to fight cancer and other diseases. In short, our weakened immune system makes us more vulnerable to diseases than when we were younger.

Dr. Takashi Makinodan and his colleagues found that when they exposed mice to controlled doses of disease organisms to stimulate measurable immune system response, the response in old mice was 10 percent of that in young mice, a 90 percent decline in disease-fighting capacity.

A very exciting thing happened when old and young T cells and B cells were mixed together. The old cells became able to produce antibodies at the same rate as the young ones. The researchers also infected young mice with disease bacteria to stimulate their immune systems, then extracted some of their T cells and B cells, froze them for several months and, after thawing, injected them into old mice. Even long after receiving the injections, the old mice resisted infection with disease organisms lethal to older, unprotected mice.[7]

Wouldn't it be something if a young person could have a number of T cells and B cells frozen before his immune system becomes weakened in advancing years? Then when he got older, he could receive an injection of the T cells and B cells that had been frozen, thus stimulating his immune system so it could function with the power of a young person's immune system.

The medical profession is at last beginning to conduct research in nutrition, the role of vitamins as a means of preventing cancer, improving health, increasing energy, and prolonging life. Now for some of you, that may not seem surprising, but it is if you realize that nutrition, vitamins, minerals, body chemistry, and stress reduction have not been included in courses offered in most medical schools in the United States. Maybe then you can realize why some of us "health nuts" in preventive medicine are so exhilarated by the turn of events.

Nutritionist Simin Meydani of the U.S. Department of Agriculture reported on research on vitamin E to help the elderly strengthen their immune system and fight off disease. Volunteers were given a total of 800 international units (IU) of vitamin E. After one month, they showed a marked increase in immune responsiveness as measured by standard skin tests of immune response and test tube measurements of white blood cell response to foreign materials.

An increasing number of scientists believe that many of the deleterious effects of aging arise from the interaction of body tissues with highly reactive forms of oxygen. This is the same oxidation process that causes the flesh of a freshly cut apple to turn brown or butter to turn rancid. Cells of the immune system are among the most sensitive to oxidation in the body and are thus the first to be affected as the body's normal repair processes begin to fail with age.

Vitamin E is an antioxidant. It tracks down the reactive form of oxygen and neutralizes it so that it can no longer cause damage. It also can stimulate the action of immune system components that are themselves antioxidants.[8] When the trace mineral selenium, an antioxidant alone, is added, the ability of vitamin E to work as an antioxidant is greatly increased.

Let me give you an example of the danger of oxidation. When a person has surgery for cancer, the surgeon is very well aware that opening up the body to oxygen will cause a rapid growth of cancer cells.

Vitamin C has long been known as an antioxidant that protects cell membranes against the damage of oxidation. One of the most important functions of vitamin C is the synthesis, formation, and maintenance of collagen for the body. Collagen is the glue that holds the tissues and organs together in the body. It is the substance in the bones that provides the toughness and flexibility and prevents brittleness. Without collagen, the body would just disintegrate or dissolve away.[9]

The 1937 Nobel Prize winner in medicine and the discoverer of vitamin C, Albert Szent-Gyorgyi, M.D., writes, "Cancer is, according to my findings, a breakdown of the normal mechanism of the cell, and so it follows that there is the less chance for a breakdown, the better the condition of the whole mechanism. My feeling is that ascorbic acid helps to keep the living machinery in good shape."[10]

I wish that vitamin C could be called something else, like the C Factor in health. Even calling it ascorbic acid doesn't seem sufficient for all the value it has for our health. We need vitamin C for many more reasons than the prevention of scurvy. Ascorbic acid, vitamin C, is vital for the functioning of the immune system as well as for producing collagen.

One problem with vitamin C is that it is water soluble, and any form of stress, physical or emotional trauma, will cause a loss of vitamin C through the urine. There are no places to store it, which means the body requires a continuous supply. Of all the thousands of animals in the world, only human beings, monkeys, and guinea pigs do not produce their own vitamin C and have to depend on foodstuffs or supplements for their supply.[11]

The immune response depends on the level of ascorbic acid in the blood and tissues. If the ascorbic acid levels are too low, the B cells and macrophages will not attack, ingest, or digest the invading forces. It has been reported that an intake of 5,000 milligrams (mg) or 10,000 mg of vitamin C daily will greatly increase the rate of production of B cells.[12]

Medical research is now reporting that some foods seem to be natural inhibitors of cancer. A study in the *Journal of the National Cancer Institute* that examined avoidable risks of cancer reported that dietary factors were found to comprise the largest single category of modifiable risks. The investigators suggested that 35 percent of all cancer deaths might be related to diet. Changes in diet might allow a 90 percent reduction in deaths due to stomach and large bowel cancers, and a 50 percent reduction in deaths due to uterine and breast cancers.[13]

Vitamin A, or beta carotene, is found to be helpful in fighting the development of tumors and some forms of skin cancer and in protecting against lung cancer. Deep green, orange, or yellow fruit and vegetables contain the largest amounts of vitamin A. Good sources are green peas, broccoli, brussels sprouts, asparagus, carrots, and oranges.

Vitamin C is associated with lower risks of cancer of the stomach and esophagus and is found in citrus fruit, broccoli, brussels sprouts, asparagus, cauliflower, green peppers, peas, raspberries, and strawberries.

Whole grain foods that are high in fiber decrease the risk of cancer in the colon. Also, research is showing that the risk of colon and rectal cancer decreased in proportion to the consumption of dietary vitamin D and calcium. This finding was reported in 1985 in the prestigious British medical journal *Lancet.* In the same year, researchers from Memorial Sloan-Kettering Cancer Center, reporting in *The New England Journal of Medicine,* found that abnormal cell proliferation in the bowel could be inhibited by supplementary calcium.[14]

I have dreamed of the day that science would begin to devote as much interest and research money exploring the secrets of the immune system and the healing warriors within as we have spent on outer space. The development of monoclonal antibodies is one of the great breakthroughs in medical science of the past fifty years.

I have read everything I can on the immune system to see how it works to keep us well and heal us. I have often wondered why, when a person goes to a physician for a health checkup, the person's immune system is never even questioned or tested to ascertain the strength, numbers, and internal balance of the T cells and the B cells. Have you ever had an immune check by a physician and then been told what to take and what to do to strengthen and enhance your healing warriors within? An examination of the immune system should become a routine procedure, especially after a severe crisis in a person's life.

The obvious way to keep the immune system healthy is to live a life-style of positive wellness such as I am suggesting in this book. Here are a few specific suggestions that will help you maintain that life-style.

1. Avoid chronic stress and exhaustion.

2. Stop smoking.
3. Be monogamous.
4. Seek help immediately during and after a severe emotional crisis in your life. Don't stifle your emotions. Hang loose emotionally.
5. Develop good nutritional habits.

I do the following for myself. I write them, acknowledging that this plan has not been established scientifically as medical truth and, therefore, not recommending them to you. Here is what I take daily as a preventive measure to help me keep a healthy immune system:

- vitamin C, or ascorbic acid—5,000 mg (10,000 mg under acute stress)
- vitamin E, d-alpha tocopherol—800 IU
- zinc—15 mg
- beta carotene—25,000 IU
- selenium—25 micrograms (*Note:* This supplement is toxic and could be fatal in large doses, so be careful.)
- pantothenic acid—200 mg
- multivitamin and mineral supplement
- calcium—1,000 mg
- magnesium—500 mg

As research continues to unravel the mysteries of the immune system, we may see the day when the art of staying well will become the science of staying well because of what we have learned about protecting, strengthening, and healing through the healing warriors of the immune system.

NOTES

1. Irving Oyle, *The New American Medicine Show* (Santa Cruz, Calif.: Unity Press, 1979).
2. William Stockton, "A New Clue in the Cancer Mystery," *The New York Times Magazine,* April 2, 1978.
3. Dolores King, "When Your Immune System Fails," *Parade Magazine,* June 18, 1987.
4. Ibid.
5. Leon Jaroff, "Stop That Germ!" *Time,* May 23, 1988.
6. King, Ibid.
7. Leonard Hayflick, "What We Are Discovering About Your Body's Amazing Immune System," *Executive Health* (November 1978).
8. Thomas H. Maugh II, "Vitamin E Might Help Elderly Battle Disease, Study Indicates," *Los Angeles Times,* October 2, 1988.
9. Irwin Stone, *The Healing Factor* (New York: Grossett & Dunlap, 1972).
10. Albert Szent-Gyorgyi, "On a Substance That Can Make Us Sick (If We Do Not Eat It)," *Executive Health* 13 (June 1977).
11. Stone, Ibid.
12. R. H. Yonemoto, P. B. Chretien, and T. H. Fehniger, "Enhanced Lymphocy to Blastogenesis by Oral Ascorbic Acid," *American Society of Clinical Oncology* 288 (1976).
13. Stuart M. Berger, "How What You Can Eat Can Add Years to Your Life," *Parade Magazine,* March 30, 1986.
14. Ibid.

CHAPTER FOUR

HOW TO PREVENT
CORONARY HEART DISEASE

One February on a flight to Chicago from Phoenix, I noticed the deep tan of the man sitting next to me. I asked him if he got his tan on a vacation in Arizona. He replied, "I've been on a vacation of sorts visiting my brother who lives on the Colorado River. The main reason I was on this vacation was to recuperate from my second coronary artery bypass surgery. I thought the first bypass would do the job, but then I collapsed on Christmas Day. I was rushed to the hospital for my second operation. I was really scared this time. I'm fifty-three years old, and I don't think I'd live through a third bypass."

We chatted for a while about his exercise routine and his diet, but he was very discouraged because he had been religiously doing his exercises and following his diet before his collapse. When I asked him what he did for a living in Chicago, his eyes lit up, and he replied, "I'm glad you asked me that because I believe my stress at work has something to do with my heart problem. No one has ever asked me about my stress at work. I am a superintendent of a very large plant in Chicago that manufactures highly volatile, explosive chemicals. If I don't keep a close watch on all the gauges and closely supervise the men, well, one mistake could blow up the whole plant and a couple of blocks of Chicago."

I was stunned. This man's stress response was one of constant "red alert" because his body was flooded with "fight or flight" hormones from the adrenals, keeping him in a state of chronic stress that created his coronary heart disease.

I recommended that he insist on a less stressful job or find a new one that would not put so much stress on his heart and coronary vessels. His job was slowly killing him, and a third coronary bypass was not the answer.

My friend was very relieved and began to relax. He said, "I was already becoming tense and fearful about returning to work. You're right. That job is a killer. In fact, it is so stressful that now that I think more about it, it takes a new employee at least two weeks before he can keep his lunch down."

Flanders Dunbar, a pioneer in psychosomatic medicine, studied the emotional characteristics of patients with certain diseases, such as hypertension and heart ailments. Dunbar's findings disclosed that among heart attack patients, men outnumbered women by six to one. She labeled coronary disease as the "middle-aged man's disease." She observed that the coronary prone have great difficulty sharing responsibility and find it hard to get along with their superiors. Many of them are self-made men or highly trained professionals. Their overriding personality trait is one of "compulsive striving." They would rather die than fail. The tougher things become, and the more unhappy they become, the harder they work.[1] Does this sound like anyone you know?

Flanders Dunbar was describing the driven perfectionist who was most likely raised with conditional love and the fear of rejection "if I'm not very careful or perfect." A perfectionist is programmed with a lot of "shoulds," "oughts," and "woulds." I "should" be perfect. You "should" be perfect. The world "should" be perfect. No matter how much a perfectionist accomplishes in life, no matter how many goals are achieved, the perfectionist is never satisfied or receives the psychological pay-off of feeling good about what has been accomplished. The reason is that somehow parents always received the credit when the child finally did something right for a change. I have never understood why parents demand perfection of their children when they are so imperfect.

To be raised with conditional love, to have to keep proving your self-worth all the time, keeps you from learning to trust what you think and feel about yourself. Consequently, you can never really trust anyone else in your life. That is why there is a need to control other people and events so as to make the world more secure for you. It makes it very difficult to share responsibility with others.

Perfectionism is a destructive illusion. Even if you consider yourself a perfectionist, haven't you already made at least one mistake in life? If you have already "goofed" and made at least one or two mistakes, then you are not perfect, and you will never be perfect. So relax, give up the tyranny of the "shoulds," "oughts," and "woulds," and accept yourself as you are. Give yourself credit for a change!

Our society is programming people to develop coronary heart disease by pushing them to become aggressive, competitive, and obsessed with being "number one"—even if being "number one" may mean being the first person on the block to have a coronary and make it in the obituary column of the local newspaper.

As women enter the world of work and face all its pressures, they are truly catching up with men. Their rate of coronary heart disease now equals that of their fellow male executives.

Television commercials and magazine advertisements have portrayed a stockbroker, representing a particular stock brokerage firm, racing over high hurdles in order to win for you by handling your financial future. The face is set with the grim, tense lines of a driven, competitive man. But why would you want your investments handled by that stockbroker who may be dead from a coronary within a very short time?

How big a killer is coronary heart disease? In a single year, diseases of the heart and blood vessels will kill far more Americans than died in World Wars I and II and the Korean and Vietnam wars, according to the figures released by the American Heart Association during its annual science writers' forum in New Orleans on January 17, 1988.

During the four major wars of this century, 636,282 Americans were killed. In 1985, 991,332 Americans died of heart attacks, strokes, and other blood vessel diseases. Heart attacks alone killed 540,800 people, accounting for 26 percent of the 2,084,000 deaths that year. By comparison, 407,318 Americans died in World War II.

I don't believe that coronary bypass surgery, heart transplants, and artificial hearts are the answers to coronary heart disease. The prevention of heart disease and strokes is an idea whose time has come. There are ways we can learn how to stay well in an uptight world without having a heart attack.

One of the problems of developing a program for preventing coronary heart disease is that researchers get caught in the trap of oversimplifying and overstating their research results, thus excluding other valid research findings. I want to give you an overview of the results of research that will help you understand the interconnectedness of nutrition, cholesterol, exercise, smoking, personality, behavior, stress factors, and emotional factors as they pertain to health and prevention of coronary heart disease.

The medical research community has informed us that if we reduce excessive intake of cholesterol, stop smoking, keep our blood pressure under control, reduce salt intake, keep weight down, and get physical exercise, we would greatly help prevent coronary heart disease.

The good news is that since 1950 the death rate from cardiovascular disease has *fallen by 40 percent* in the United States. The death rate has dropped more than 29 percent just in the years from 1968 to 1978. The medical research community has cited changes in life-style as a major factor that cut the risks. Some ways that people can take control and reduce the risk factors in their lives include the following:

1. Reduce cholesterol levels in the blood.
2. Give up cigarettes.
3. Control blood pressure.
4. Exercise.

A greater decline in heart attack incidence was found among younger men who are likely to have made life-style changes early in life.[2]

However, the picture of the primary coronary risk factors is complicated by a story I heard about the chairman of the Diet-Heart Committee of the American Medical Association (AMA) who was to present his recommendations for a very expensive, long-term evaluation of the restriction of animal fat in the diet to an AMA meeting in June 1967. He had followed his own recommended low-fat regimen for years; he had kept slim, exercised regularly, and in every way followed his own advice on how to prevent heart attacks. Unfortunately, he was unable to attend that meeting because he was in a hospital recovering from a coronary thrombosis.

Next, I heard of what happened to Robert S. Eliot, M.D., who directs the National Center of Preventive and Stress Medicine at St. Luke's Hospital in Phoenix, Arizona, where I live. In his own words he tells what happened:

At age 44, as I stood at the podium giving a learned lecture on managing emergencies of the heart, I had a heart attack. Happily, it was the kind everyone should have if they must have one, a mild one and in a hospital. From the time the elephant sat on my chest until I was securely monitored in a coronary care unit, only 20 minutes had passed. But as I looked up from the wrong side of the sheets, I had to ask myself, "What happened?"

I had none of the classic risk factors for heart disease. I didn't smoke, wasn't fat, didn't have diabetes, didn't have high blood pressure, didn't have high cholesterol. My father had lived to 79, and my mother was still alive at 85, both free of heart disease. Plus, I was a cardiologist, an expert in heart disease.

During my three months of recuperation, I took time— for the first time in my life—to try to understand what made me tick. I came to realize that what had almost killed me was an overindulgence in work with the accompanying stress, what I perceived to be losing situations, a joyless struggle. You see, I had fixed in my head that by age 40 I *must* be Chief of Cardiology at a major medical center. Running a little behind schedule, I picked up the pace. Along the way I ignored warning signals which my body was sending out. I had no time for family and friends, for exercise and leisure. My life had become a blur of overachievement. But now I had to ask myself: Is it worth dying for?[3]

Dr. Eliot developed the personality profile of what he calls the hot reactors who react so strongly their bodies produce large quantities of stress hormones that lead to great changes in the cardiovascular system, including remarkable rises in blood pressure. They are pressure cookers without safety valves, literally stirring in their own juices.

Remember Hans Selye's statement: "It's not the amount of stress you have; it's how you respond to it."

The great Canadian physician, Sir William Osler, said, "It is not the delicate neurotic person who is prone to angina, but the robust, the vigorous in mind and body, the keen ambitious man, the individual whose engine is always at 'full speed ahead'—the well set man of from forty-five to fifty-five years of age, with military bearing, iron gray hair, and florid complexion." He was essentially describing the hero of the American industrial society.

I have found that this type of person has poor eating habits, skips meals, drinks too much alcohol, has no time for physical exercise, and uses coffee, soft drinks, and cigarettes to provide energy. Sleep is usually a problem, and though the person may be very successful, he doesn't know how to slow down, relax, and play without turning the play into a competitive contest. This man is very well educated and knowledgeable in the areas of life that are important to his career, but he cannot express his feelings. If asked what he *feels,* he will tell you what he *thinks*. If the man is struck down with a heart attack, the blow to his self-esteem is catastrophic. Here is a big problem he can't solve in a few minutes. He makes an impossible patient and drives everyone around him crazy. And if he is a physician, he is even worse! He vacillates between unprovoked outbursts of anger and despair, which often lead to a black depression in which he gives up his will to live. The other reaction is to pretend to be so positive as to deny he had a heart attack. As soon as he is back on his feet, he tries to prove to everyone that he's fine. He ignores the physician's guidelines for his recovery and resumes his driven pace as soon as possible until he is struck down for his "final count."

Drs. Meyer Friedman and Ray Rosenman have searched for factors other than the usual six coronary risk factors. In their book *Type A Behavior and Your Heart,*[4] they describe two personality types: Type A who has a good chance of coronary heart disease, and Type B who rarely suffers from coronary heart disease.

Type A personality, whether male or female, is characterized by intense drive, aggressiveness, ambition, competitiveness, free-floating hostility, a chronic sense of time urgency, and a "hurry sickness." Under pressure of the hurry sickness, people often try to do more than one thing at the same time, such as taking a shower and brushing their teeth. I was drawn to this article in a Sunday issue of the *Los Angeles Times:*

> After a long, hard day at the office, New York market researcher Judith Langer likes to unwind at home in front of the television set. But she doesn't just sit there watching TV. She also eats dinner, plays with her cat, scans the newspaper, and chats on the phone with a friend—all at the same time. Her only regret is that "I haven't figured out anything (to do) with my feet."
>
> If Langer's way of relaxing seems decidedly unrelaxed, it's only a sign of the times. In an age of high living standards, longer vacations, faster transportation and supermarkets stuffed with convenience items, Americans somehow have wound up feeling more harried than ever.[5]

Psychologists, time management experts, and other observers point out that too many people are as busy off the job as on. Used to doing three things at once at the office, they try to maintain the same pace away from it. Harried, hurried, and haunted, they rush through their lives under the tyranny of the clock in an Age of Haste.

In going to Maui for seminars for dentists and their wives, I've found it very revealing to see how time bound the couples are when they arrive. "How long did it take to get from your house?" "When will the luggage arrive?" "Hurry up and get in line for the car rental so we can begin to relax." One dentist from Pittsburgh could not shut off his mind; he continually worried about his practice. I told him he was in Maui to hang loose. Two days later he said, "I tried to hang loose. But yesterday I called my office, and no one answered the phone! Hanging loose is impossible!" I asked him what time he called his office, and when he told me, I asked if his office is usually open at 9:00 P.M. on Friday. He had forgotten about the five-hour time difference between Maui and Pittsburgh.

In contrast, a Type B personality is able to hang loose emotionally. He feels good about himself and does not need the approval of others to feel satisfaction. He is able to work and then let go of work. He is not always looking at his watch. Meyer Friedman told a seminar audience in Portland, Oregon, that since he has already had his coronary, he has permission not to be overly concerned by time, so he no longer wears a wristwatch.

Life is not by numbers, unlike the feelings of a Type A personality. Type B is more interested in the quality of life. He does not always have to be first. He is also able to delegate responsibility. He enjoys time out to think and be creative. He can relax and not feel guilty about not doing anything. The Type B personality enjoys many aspects of life that are not work oriented. Friedman says that this relaxed attitude toward life is a key factor. If a real Type B person ever has a heart attack and dies, Friedman and Rosenman will pay for his funeral. They have yet to pay for a funeral.

Now, at this point, many Type A personalities are justifying their driven outlook and competitiveness because it's the Type A person who gets things done and is the most successful. Not true, says the latest research. A Type B person has the inner security to think, plan, and not be rushed into a decision because of time or fear of making a mistake. Plus, he also lives longer and actually makes more money during his lifetime.

Since emotions, mind, spirit, body, and environment are so interconnected, Type A behavior creates a very disruptive and dangerous state of hormonal imbalance within the organism. The stress response under which the Type A personality lives, when it becomes chronic, causes the sympathetic nervous system to secret adrenaline, hormones of norepinephrine and epinephrine that cause arteries to constrict and raise blood pressure. Epinephrine is a fear hormone, and norepinephrine is an anger hormone. They keep the body in a state of "red alert" since they feel that a catastrophe is coming. Type A people secret almost twice as much norepinephrine, the "fight" hormone, as do Type B personalities. It has become increasingly suspect as a major hormone in causing coronary heart disease. In fact, all the biochemical abnormalities observed in most coronary patients are also found in Type A people decades before they fall prey to coronary heart disease.

Since the time of their book (1974), Friedman and Rosenman have questioned three hundred business executives and seventy physicians treating coronary patients. They asked what these people thought might have precipitated a heart attack in a friend or patient. Three-fourths of the executives said they thought having excessive competitive drive and too many deadlines had triggered heart attacks in their friends. To the researchers' considerable surprise, approximately three-fourths of the physicians responded similarly, even though the medical journals they were reading invariably cited dietary habits, smoking, and lack of exercise as sole factors in producing coronary heart disease.[6]

Accountants were one of the next groups studied since their work rises and falls in intensity, from slow times to the rushed times of closing out clients' yearly books and coping with income taxes from March to April 15. The accountants were asked to keep detailed diaries of what they ate. They were examined in Friedman and Rosenman's office twice a month, and cholesterol levels were measured during slack periods and times of heavy pressure. The doctors discovered that the two significant cholesterol peaks occurred during the two periods the accountants were pressured for time; there was an overall falling off of those levels in months of more routine work.[7] If the accountants had to go on from acute stress to chronic stress—in other words, if they continued working at the intensity level of their two peak times—they could very well be subject to serious, even fatal, coronary disease problems.

In talking about the cholesterol factor in preventing heart disease with "my son, the doctor," Danny (an M.D. in internal medicine in Tucson, Arizona), I learned that our bodies produce 75 percent of our cholesterol, but our diet is responsible for only 25 percent of it. Dietary factors alone are not sufficient in and of themselves to prevent cardiovascular disease.

The liver manufactures most of the body's cholesterol. During chronic stress, the continuous flooding of the body with the adaptive stress hormones can have serious effects on a person's health. The adrenals release corticoids into the bloodstream that can, over extended periods of time, raise the blood pressure and cause serious kidney damage. The proinflammatory corticoids can also cause tears in the walls of arteries. (Leaky arteries can be harmful to your health!) Chronic stress continues to release cholesterol from your liver and large intestines at the time the artery walls are being constructed. The tears in the walls of the arteries are repaired by cholesterol plaque, which leads to hardening of the arteries or arteriosclerosis. If some of the cholesterol plaque breaks off from the arterial wall, a blockage in the main arteries to the heart can occur and produce a coronary heart attack.

During normal activities or during a short period of acute stress, the liver controls the amount of corticoids in the blood, but during chronic stress, the liver's control mechanism is bypassed, which permits high concentrations of proinflammatory corticoids to circulate throughout the body.[8] Not only do the hormones from the adrenals overwhelm the body during chronic stress, but the pituitary gland oversecretes hormones that cause the whole endocrine system to be overworked. Also, secretion of too much insulin from the pancreas creates blood sugar imbalance and can lead to diabetes.

In 1969, the United States cut back severely on the funding for the space program. The loss of a job was disastrous for many of the highly trained technical specialists. How many jobs are available for people whose training and expertise have been geared toward the project of sending vehicles to the moon? The effects of the job losses caused high rates of divorce and alcohol consumption. There was an unusual number of sudden death heart attacks among young men who had no prior history of coronary heart disease. The rate ran 50 percent higher than usual for men in their age group.

In the autopsies, it was found that the heart muscle had a type of damage not usually associated with heart attacks. It seemed as though the heart had been thrown into overdrive by excessive amounts of the "fight" hormone of the adrenals, norepinephrine. The heart was stimulated to be on "red alert" until the area in the frontal cortex of the brain, which controls the heart rhythms and contractions, may have been overloaded, causing the heart muscle to go into fatal fibrillation.[9]

If a loss of a job can cause a sudden death heart attack, then it is obvious that the sudden loss of a loved one through death can cause death from a broken heart. In working with people who are in a state of shock and grief over the loss of a loved one, I have seen the grieving person experience rapid weight loss, depression, loss of interest in life, memory problems, sleep disorders, poor eating habits, and an accelerated aging process. Physical health rapidly declines, and soon there are a series of physical illnesses and often, within the next six months to a year, a fatal coronary or stroke. Yet as serious a health threat as this is, few people receive adequate grief counseling to help them live through the experience.

Colin Parkes in his book *Bereavement* has researched the premature death of the remaining loved one and pointed out that the increased mortality among the bereaved is especially high during the first six months after the loss. This finding clearly implies that the increase in mortality in widows and widowers is not due to the fact that these individuals are simply too sick to remarry, because most of the sudden deaths occur before there would have been sufficient time to remarry. In 75 percent of the cases Parkes studied, the cause of death in bereaved individuals was coronary thrombosis or arteriosclerosis.

Dr. James Lynch wrote a powerful book called *The Broken Heart*. It is about life and death—love, companionship, and health—and loneliness that can break the human heart. Lynch documents the fact that reflected in our hearts is a biological basis for our need to form loving human relationships. If we fail to fulfill that need, our health is in peril. He states, "Since human dialogue is the elixir of life, the ultimate decision we must make is simple; we must either learn to live together or increase our chances of prematurely dying alone."[10]

We have become a nation of socially fragmented individuals. For the most part, we have lost a sense of community. To how many people could you turn to pour out your grief and inner pain? How many family members live in the same town? Too many of us suffer from a high degree of social isolation and loneliness in our lives. Often both husband and wife work, and after-work hours are so busy that we are strangers even to those to whom we are married. We are all suffering from loneliness.

I hope these suggestions about how to have a healthy heart will prevent someone from having a heart attack or stroke. If what I say next helps one person, then it has been worthwhile writing this book.

First, let's look at traditional risk factors for the prevention of heart disease.

If you did not have any cholesterol in your body, you would die because cholesterol is a very necessary substance for the building of all membranes. Cholesterol travels in the bloodstream attached to proteins called lipoproteins. Now science has distinguished two types of cholesterol based on their density. The villain of cholesterol in heart disease is low-density lipoproteins (LDL). These molecules travel through the blood vessels leaving life-threatening deposits within the walls of arteries. Most of the cholesterol in the blood is LDL.

The good cholesterol, high-density lipoproteins (HDL), exists in smaller amounts in the bloodstream. The good guys, HDL, work as garbage collectors and scavengers, sucking up excess cholesterol and inhibiting LDL deposits on the walls of arteries.

The basic cholesterol question has been this: Would lowering a person's cholesterol levels actually reduce that person's chance of developing coronary heart disease? The proof came as the result of a study begun in 1972 by more than a dozen specialized medical clinics in the United States, Canada, Israel, and the Soviet Union. The research, designed to find out whether lowering cholesterol levels was effective, was conducted on 3,800 men who had particularly high cholesterol levels but were free from heart disease when the study began. Six times a day for seven years the men took either a placebo or a drug called cholestyramine, which lowers cholesterol levels.

Results showed that the group receiving cholestyramine had an *8 percent* greater reduction in cholesterol levels than the group receiving the placebo, and it also had a *19 percent* lower rate of heart attacks and deaths from heart disease. In addition, the study showed that the drug was particularly beneficial in reducing the amount of LDL cholesterol. Results from other studies indicating that a high rate of LDL increases the risk of heart disease were thus confirmed. The good news is that higher amounts of HDL cholesterol actually lower the risk of coronary artery disease.[11]

The *New England Journal of Medicine* reported on a Finnish study over a five-year period in which four thousand Finlanders were given a drug called gemfibrozil. Those treated with the drug suffered only two-thirds as many heart attacks and cardiac-related deaths. After three years of treatment, that fraction dropped to less than half. This is the largest decrease in coronary disease in any study so far.

The Finnish study makes clear that treatment to lessen the risk of heart attacks should concentrate as much on raising the HDL cholesterol levels as on lowering dangerous LDL cholesterol levels. This conclusion alone could point to more exciting research in this area that could result in not only longer life but also better life for thousands.[12]

Now, what are some of the things a person can do to raise the amount of the "good guys"—HDL cholesterol—which help to prevent artery clogging?

Regular exercise has been coming to the forefront as a means of increasing the HDL cholesterol levels in the blood. George V. Mann, after examining the four major lines of evidence that refute the simplified "diet-heart" link, concluded that there is considerably more evidence linking exercise as a more critical variable than dietary factors alone, and he pointed out the evidence suggesting that fit and active people are spared the complications of arteriosclerosis.[13]

One of the most convincing evidences of the value of exercise is provided by a study of sixteen thousand Harvard graduates over a period of twenty years, during which time the occupational and recreational exercise habits were documented and the frequency of heart attacks and death was recorded. The men who engaged in regular, vigorous exercises had half the number of heart attacks and half the heart death incidence of the sedentary men.

We know that regular exercise burns up calories, which helps to lower total cholesterol and increases the production of HDL cholesterol. Exercise also helps reduce weight; thus, blood pressure is lowered.[14]

I have recommended exercise for depressed people since depression slows down the large motor muscle activity. Exercise forces large muscle activity and helps break some of the power of depression. Most of all, the person ceases to be a victim of helplessness and hopelessness. Have you ever seen a depressed 100-yard dash runner?

The question being asked is, What kind of exercise? As a nation we have experienced a physical fitness craze of jogging, marathons, and "pumping iron"—women as well as men. There was a creed of "no pain, no gain" in physical fitness. Now there is a call for moderation in exercise because too much exercise may be hazardous to your health.

Even Dr. Kenneth Cooper, "Dr. Aerobic," who helped start the fitness boom in 1968 with his best-seller, *Aerobics,* has changed his mind after suffering from bone fractures and heel problems. He said, "I used to believe that if some exercise was good, I thought more had to be better. I was wrong. There is a point of diminishing returns." Muscle and joint injuries in runners pushing past twenty-five miles a week have reportedly overwhelmed the staff at Cooper's clinic in Dallas, Texas.

Jim Fixx, who spurred the jogging craze with his best-selling books and who preached the running gospel that active people live longer, died of a heart attack while jogging at the age of fifty-two. Why did he die that way if being physically active reduces by about one-third the incidence of coronary disease?

For one thing, his family had a heredity of heart disease. His father had a heart attack at age thirty-five and died at forty-three of heart failure. There was also Fixx's life-style of heavy smoking and overeating before he turned to running. An autopsy revealed that Fixx had almost total blockage of one coronary artery, 80 percent blockage of the second, and 50 percent blockage of the third. Before his death, Fixx complained of exhaustion and tightness in his throat while running. These were symptoms of heart trouble, which he refused to accept, and he would not seek medical help.[15]

Needless to say, a new sanity is replacing the "no pain, no gain" fanaticism of physical exercise. The most beneficial exercises are taking long walks, riding an exercycle or bicycle, slow swimming, and working out on aerobic equipment such as a rowing machine. Remember, however, that moderation is the key. Exercise at least three times a week, try to make it fun, and change your routine so you won't get bored and quit.

Increasing the intake of vitamin C can raise the level of HDL cholesterol in the blood, according to a nutrition survey of 680 men and women over sixty years of age carried out by Tufts University in Boston. In Scotland researchers have found that vitamin C can prevent the rise in total blood cholesterol that commonly occurs in winter.

However, smoking cigarettes causes HDL cholesterol to go down, which may be one way it has been indicated that smoking causes heart disease. Also, eating large amounts of refined sugar *lowers* HDL cholesterol levels in the blood.

A blood level of cholesterol under 200 is desirable. Therefore, a level over 200 requires attention; the average heart disease victim has a cholesterol level of 160. How long has it been since you have had your physician check your cholesterol level, especially for the amount of HDL and LDL cholesterol? Remember that LDL is a better indicator of heart disease than cholesterol alone. You may have to encourage your physician to check these levels since physicians sometimes fail to test them unless asked to do so or unless a specific ailment indicates the need. Neither do they always check on a patient's diet and exercise habits, important factors in cases of high blood pressure and coronary heart disease. Furthermore, many physicians do not practice good preventive medicine in their own lives. You may save your physician's life if you ask whether his or her own cholesterol levels have been checked lately, as well as health habits of eating and exercise. The typical habits of physicians are quite unhealthy and produce considerable illness. A physician's life expectancy today is ten to fifteen years less than that of the average population.

The health revolution we are experiencing is due to public concern about health, which is illustrated by the following changes:

1. People are stopping smoking in record numbers. This reduces the risk of getting coronary heart disease and lung cancer.
2. There has been a shift from drinking hard alcohol to beer and wine or, in some cases, to no alcoholic beverages at all.
3. Caffeine in coffee and soft drinks has made people aware that too much can make them jittery, irritable, and prone to headaches. They are reducing their overall caffeine intake.
4. People are modifying dietary habits by eating less animal fats and fried foods and more fresh vegetables, fresh fruit, lean meat, fish, and chicken. Olive oil, which has no cholesterol, is being used for cooking. People have increased their consumption of fiber-rich vegetables, which include broccoli, brussels sprouts, cabbage, cauliflower, carrots, sweet potatoes, berries, tomatoes, and squash. Breakfast cereals containing bran, unpolished brown rice, and whole-grain breads have gained in popularity.

To prevent blood clots, which are directly involved in the most severe consequences of coronary heart disease, in addition to adopting the above measures as well as following an exercise program, take one aspirin a day. Experts now say aspirin could prevent more than one hundred thousand heart attacks.[16] Taking certain fish oils, notably salmon, also apparently reduces the chances of clot formation.

For preventing hypertension, diet proves to be very important. Salt is the critical factor. Studies of populations around the world where no salt is eaten except what occurs naturally in food find that blood pressure remains low throughout life. Salt is sodium chloride, and sodium, which makes up about 40 percent of salt, is essential for health. It helps regulate blood and body fluids, and it has a role in nerve impulse transmission, heart action, and the metabolizing of protein and carbohydrates.[17]

New research indicates that ordinary salt may be the only form of sodium that raises blood pressure. Thus, sodium chloride may be the culprit.[18]

The best preventive measure would be to use salt substitutes as well as herbs and spices for seasoning food.

The prevention of coronary heart disease includes learning to live with stress successfully and developing a life-style of positive wellness in regard to cholesterol, exercise, nutrition, and nonsmoking.

NOTES

1. Flanders Dunbar, *Psychosomatic Diagnosis* (New York: Paul B. Hoeben, 1943).
2. Dan Sperling, "Diet, Exercise Cut Heart Attacks by a Third," *USA Today,* April, 4, 1985.

3. Robert S. Eliot and Dennis Breo, *Is It Worth Dying For?* (New York: Bantam, 1984).
4. Meyer Friedman and Ray Rosenman, *Type A Behavior and Your Heart* (New York: Fawcett Crest, 1974).
5. A. Kent MacDougall, "Americans: Life in the Fast Lane," *Los Angeles Times,* April 17, 1983.
6. Meyer Friedman, "On Type A Behavior," *Executive Health* 18 (May 1982).
7. Ibid.
8. Kenneth R. Pelletier, *Mind as Healer, Mind as Slayer* (New York: Dell, 1977).
9. Hans Selye, "On Executive Stress," *Executive Health* 18 (October 1981).
10. James J. Lynch, *The Broken Heart* (New York: Basic Books, 1977).
11. Michael Criqui, "Up Date on Heart Disease: What Do We Know About It—And How," *Executive Health Report* 23 (November 1986).
12. Christine Gorman, "The Battle of Lipoproteins," *Time,* November 23, 1987.
13. George V. Mann, "Diet—Heart. End of an Era," *New England Journal of Medicine* 297 (1977): 644–50.
14. Albert A. Kattus, "On Exercise and Cardiovascular Health," *Executive Health* 20 (April 1984).
15. "Fitness Without Fads," *Executive Health* 21 (April 1985).
16. "Miracle Drug in the Medicine Chest," *U.S. News & World Report,* February 8, 1988.
17. Lot B. Page, "On Making Sense of Salt and Your Blood Pressure," *Executive Health* 18 (August 1982).
18. "Study Hints Table Salt May Be Only Sodium Hiking Blood Pressure," *Arizona Republic,* October 23, 1987.

CHAPTER FIVE

THE UGLY
FACE OF PAIN

"Pain, not death, is the enemy of mankind."—Bonnie Prudden.

Jeannie, my wife, tells of her experience with pain.

"It started out with a pain in my right hip. I thought it was arthritis so I took some aspirin, but the pain didn't go away. In fact, it got worse. At the grocery store the pain got so bad I could hardly finish the shopping. What's wrong with me? At first I thought my slacks were too tight and were cutting off the circulation, but then there was severe pain in the middle of my back. Was my sciatic nerve pinched?

"I tried a Valium as a muscle relaxant, and it didn't help. I thought perhaps I would have to be hospitalized, put in traction, and have all kinds of X rays taken to see if surgery would correct the problem and take away the pain.

"My mind was imagining the worst—maybe—maybe— it's bone cancer. A chill of sheer panic raced through my body. Then came the depression. I thought I wouldn't get over this in time for us to fly to London in two weeks to spend some days there before taking a cruise to Scandinavia and Russia. Tears rolled down my cheeks. We had dreamed about this trip for over two years.

"Each day the pain became worse; I could barely walk. The thought of being crippled, walking with a cane, being prematurely old, haunted me. Sleep was almost impossible. I don't know what happened. One day the pain was there, and was so intense that it made me sick to my stomach. Kenny kept asking to help me by pushing on the trigger points of muscle spasms, but I didn't believe it would help me. Finally he insisted, and since I was so desperate, I agreed.

"When Kenny pushed on a trigger point, the pain was so sharp, tears came to my eyes. Then strangely enough in the place where he had pressed with his thumb, it began to feel better! After he had located every muscle spasm, he put me through a series of stretching exercises.

"It was a miracle! In three to four days I was completely free of pain. The treatment of the muscle spasm was painful, but it was a hurt-so-good pain because I soon became pain-free."

How did this pain start with Jeannie? We live on an acre of natural desert in Paradise Valley, Arizona. Contrary to what many people think, our desert is not just drifting sand dunes, but is filled with trees, cactus, sagebrush, creosote bushes, and other types of growth. Our daughter, Jan, is a wonderful gardener, and she had been trimming trees while Jeannie dragged the tree limbs to a place where they were piled to be picked up. Jeannie has never been athletic, so she was using muscles that were not used to heavy exercise, and she had pulled the limbs by twisting her body to drag them. The muscle strain led to the development of trigger points, which caused the muscles to go into spasm with resulting pain. Other trigger points in her back, gluteal muscles, and legs were "ignited" by trigger points and spasms, which gave the effect of the muscle spasms and pain spreading.

I shudder to think what would have happened to Jeannie if I had not bought Bonnie Prudden's book, *Pain Erasure, the Bonnie Prudden Way*. Our long-awaited trip would have been a disaster. I could have taken her to one physician after another or to chiropractors. She might have been hospitalized, running up expensive medical bills for tests, and then been told there was nothing neurologically wrong with her body. Surgery could have been done, which would not have eliminated the pain. So Jeannie would have become one of the millions of chronic pain sufferers, living on antidepressants and painkillers, but still very depressed with her bright mind in a dopey chemical fog. It is difficult to understand why physicians, who are the "body" doctors, know so very little about the muscles of the body.

An article in *Newsweek* reports that the average chronic pain patient has suffered for seven years, undergone from three to five major operations, and spent from $50,000 to $100,000 on doctor bills. In between surgeries he has taken countless drugs, from tranquilizers and muscle relaxants to potent narcotics, and there is at least a fifty-fifty chance that he has acquired a drug habit along the way.[1]

Nowhere has the traditional medical model been more destructive than in the programming of the chronic pain patient to be a passive, helpless victim. The people who must live with chronic pain live on an emotional roller coaster hoping against hope for relief from pain. They undergo personality changes that are drug induced and suffer from depression and irritability. Often they drink too much alcohol. They are weighed down, not only with pain, but with guilt for not being better spouses or not being able to care for themselves and their families. They are angry and frustrated with their doctors who offer no real help. As a result, their doctors respond defensively toward them or experience frustration at not being able to help.

Albert Schweitzer wrote in *Out of My Life and Thought* about his own serious illness in his early middle years and his decision at the time that if he ever recovered, he would never forget his feelings while ill. There is a "fellowship of those who bear the mark of pain. Those outside this fellowship have great difficulty in comprehending what lies behind the pain."

Norman Cousins says that during his illness of collagen disease with its intense chronic pain, his fellow patients at the hospital would talk about matters they would never discuss with their doctors. The psychology of the seriously ill puts barriers between them and those who try to minister to them.

There was, first of all, the feeling of helplessness—a serious disease in itself. There was the subconscious fear of never being able to function normally again—and it produced a wall of separation between us and the world of open movement, open sounds, open expectations.

There was the reluctance to be thought a complainer. There was the desire not to add to the already great burden of apprehension felt by one's family; this added to the isolation.

There was the conflict between the terror of loneliness and the desire to be left alone.

There was the lack of self-esteem, the subconscious feeling perhaps that our illness was a manifestation of our inadequacy.

There was the fear that decisions were being made behind our back, that not everything was made known that we wanted to know, yet dreaded knowing. There was the morbid fear of intrusive technology, fear of being metabolized by a data base, never to regain our faces again. There was resentment of strangers who came at us with needles and vials, some of which put supposedly magic substances in our veins and others which took more of our blood than we thought we could afford to lose. There was the distress of being wheeled through white corridors to laboratories for all sorts of strange encounters with compact machines and blinking lights and whirling discs.

And then there was the utter void created by the longing—ineradicable, unremitting, pervasive—for warmth of human contact. A warm smile and an outstretched hand were valued even above the offerings of modern science, but the latter were far more accessible than the former.[2]

There are two kinds of pain: acute and chronic. Acute pain is of short duration, such as the pain you experience when you touch a cactus spine. It hurts right now, but taking out the cactus spine reduces the pain quickly. Acute pain is a valuable warning system in telling a person that something is wrong and something needs to be done to take care of it, as in the case of a toothache. Modern dentistry is so advanced that the pain is eliminated with little discomfort.

Chronic pain is very different. It isn't the simple pain of an infected or a broken tooth. Most chronic pain is caused by a condition in the muscles. True, disease is responsible for some of it, but just daily living with stress is the usual cause. Painkillers don't kill that type of pain.

Muscle spasms, such as Jeannie had, won't show up on any X ray. A healthy muscle contracts when it is in use and relaxes when the work is over. Muscles are affected by stress as the person prepares for action, for fight or flight. This consists of an automatic instinctive bracing of skeletal muscles in preparation for action. It is the "red alert" time for the muscles. If the stress is not relieved and the muscles allowed to relax again, the muscles affected by stress stay contracted and tense. After a time, a muscle under constant tension will go into spasm and be unable to relax at all. If you don't exercise regularly, as in Jeannie's case, your body is more susceptible to the effects of stress than if you were active. Tension builds up faster in muscles that are weak and stiff from lack of exercise. Also, when muscles have had prior damage, weakness in muscle tone results, with an increased likelihood of muscle tension and muscle spasms.

From childhood to adulthood, there are constant emotional conflicts and hurts. What are people to do with the energy from these emotions? Some, perhaps far too few, react by discharging the emotion in anger or tears or by acting out the emotion physically. Far too many of us react by swallowing our emotions and suppressing them, internalizing that energy in muscles and organs of the body, or denying the emotional energy that later surfaces in some physical or emotional illness. Children may react with stomachaches, abnormal fears, asthma attacks, skin rashes, or headaches. The unresolved emotional conflicts with their undissipated energy are often locked into the "armor plating" of their muscles and joints and in the subconscious mind.

Emotional conflict with its field of energy thus plays a major role in chronic pain. The denial of emotional pain often resurfaces as chronic physical pain. When you awaken in the morning with tense muscles, you feel just as tired as when you went to sleep. Often your hands are clenched, and your jaw muscles are sore from gritting your teeth. When you get out of bed, you feel as though you had worked all night.

Bonnie Prudden discovered myotherapy when she was thirty years old. She was climbing a mountain with friends and awoke the second morning with a very painful stiff neck. Because she had fallen from a bucking horse years earlier, she often had a stiff neck. Dr. Hans Kraus, a member of the party, looked at her lopsided head and knew she wouldn't be much good on a climb in her condition. He placed a thumb on the back of her neck and pressed so hard her knees buckled. That didn't stop him because he knew what he was doing; he meant to squash the knot—whatever it took. Mountain climbers are fanatics, and nothing must get in the way of a climb. Bonnie said she was hard put not to cry, but when he let up, her head was on straight. There was no pain at all, so off they went on a magnificent climb.[3]

The word *myotherapy* is made up of *myo,* which means

"muscle," and *therapy*, which means "service to." Unlike the acupuncture points used in pressure therapy, the trigger points in myotherapy are different in each person. Accidents suffered in childhood, poor posture, certain diseases, reaction to stress—all contribute to each person's unique trigger point makeup.

Bonnie Prudden says that we don't know exactly what a trigger point is. A trigger point won't show up in an autopsy, but it is a highly irritable spot in a muscle that contributes to pain. Evidently, trigger points are laid down in muscles all through life. Any number of things, such as a fall, blow, strain, or sprain, can insult the muscles.

A trigger point lies quietly in a muscle until the physical and emotional climate is right, and then it fires. Its firing throws the muscle into spasm. This causes pain and the autonomic nervous system comes complete with plans for handling pain. It sends a spasm to the affected area to protect it against whatever is threatening. When the spasm sent by the nervous system reaches the designated area, it further tightens the spasm already present. That hurts! Another pain message shoots back to headquarters predictably followed by yet more spasms. This phenomenon is called "splinting." We now have a spasm-pain-spasm cycle in effect, and until it is broken, the pain will continue unabated. As the pain continues, so will the splinting. This shortens the muscles and holds them in a foreshortened condition, which not only causes pain, but interferes with function, posture, and balance. If the cycle is maintained long enough, the muscles may remain permanently shortened.[4]

The spasm-pain-spasm can also develop satellite trigger points in the muscles. For example, if there is a trigger point in the trapezius muscle across the back and if the spasms continue, nearby areas will develop satellite trigger points that are also painful.

Prudden asks these very basic questions of people in pain:

1. Where do you hurt?
2. What were your sports in school?
3. Have you had or been in any accidents?
4. Have you had any operations?
5. Have you any children? How were they born? [Women get these.]
6. What medications are you on?
7. What were your occupations?
8. When was the first time you had the pain and what happened?[5]

It is extremely important to discover and eliminate, if at all possible, the precipitating and perpetuating factors for the muscle spasms that cause chronic pain. Having myotherapy to eliminate trigger points is rather useless until the causes have been dealt with. Symptom relief is not helpful or healing.

Too much continuous stress response is the number one precipitating factor in chronic pain from muscle spasms. There are days when half the people I see in therapy are experiencing muscle spasm pain. For a few of them, the pain is of recent origin, but too many have lived in chronic pain for years, going from physician to physician, and chiropractor to chiropractor, pill to pill, but with no relief, little hope of relief, and a chronic depression from the pain.

People are surprised when I ask, "How long have you been in pain?" From my experience, however, I suspect pain when I see a person sitting stiff as though afraid to move.

When the person describes the location of the pain, the surprise is even greater when I put my thumb on a trigger point, and the person jumps in pain and says, "You've found it!" Then I continue locating trigger points from the neck down into the back muscles, if that is the location of the pain. Then I'll begin the same procedure on the other side of the neck and back. The person will say, "I don't have any pain on that side of my body." Yet I often locate a trigger point that is ready to fire off a muscle spasm very soon.

After the trigger point therapy, I teach the individual exercises to stretch the muscles so they won't go back into spasm, and I recommend the purchase of *Pain Erasure, the Bonnie Prudden Way*. If the person needs more expert treatment, I recommend someone who is trained in myotherapy.

The next area I explore is the amount of stress-activating events in the person's life: what changes have occurred, how the person reacted to the changes, sleep patterns, eating habits, medications, vitamin and mineral supplements, exercise or lack of exercise, injuries to the body, surgeries, and a description in the person's own words of his energy level, unresolved emotional difficulties, and problems with allergies, among other things.

Most of the people I see with muscle spasm pain are physically exhausted. They are the legion of the tired. Accompanying the exhaustion is a fatiguing depression from chronic stress. The first thing I recommend to such a person is *no exercise,* except for a short walk if the walk is not too tiring. Exercising with muscle spasms is a sure way to increase the strength and number of muscle spasms in the body.

Muscle spasms may indicate that the body is low on calcium and magnesium. If you ever have a leg cramp at night so severe that it causes you to jump out of bed to release it, you may have a calcium deficiency. During stress, the water-soluble vitamins, such as vitamin C and the B complex vitamins, are washed out through the urine. They need to be supplemented. Drinking alcohol also flushes out the B complex vitamins. Potassium loss will be a factor for exhausted slow oxidizers. Low potassium disturbs the smooth functioning of muscles, including heart muscles. A diet high in fat, refined sugar, and over-salted food is high in sodium and low in potassium and can lead to a deficiency. Also, having diarrhea or using diuretics or laxatives increases potassium loss. Good sources of potassium include bananas, citrus fruit, and green, leafy vegetables.

Muscle spasms can develop from skeletal inadequacies. One leg being shorter than the other can cause the body to be out of balance. The shorter leg puts the body at a tilt, which starts off a chain reaction in the body. The lumbar spine is then tilted toward the shorter leg, and compensatory scoliosis turns the shoulder, creating a commonly overlooked source of low back pain. A foot pad for the shorter leg will often correct the problem because the pelvis and shoulders will then be level. Most important, the spine will be straight.

Phantom pain from the amputation of a limb can be caused by muscle spasms above the area of amputation. Shin splints in the legs are muscle spasms underneath the shin bone, and they can be quickly released with trigger therapy.

How does a person do myotherapy and find trigger points? I use my finger to search out trigger points in the area of the body that is involved in pain. (Bonnie Prudden's book provides a guide as to where trigger points are located.) The person will let me know if I have found a trigger point! I then press down with my thumb and count to seven, then slowly release. If it is a new trigger point, then it is what Jeannie calls a hurt-so-good pain, because the pain is sharp but the relief from the muscle spasm is so welcome. After working through the muscle spasms, I have the person do a series of stretching exercises so the muscles won't go back into spasm. Taking a hot shower or using hot moist heat packs followed by rubbing in "Icy Hot" ointment is very helpful.

You can use a firm bed, a table, or even the floor to work on a person. The elbow is often used on the "hip pocket" trigger point in the gluteus maximus. This is a favorite trigger point for most back pain.

People who have had chronic pain for a long time, with muscle spasms as a way of life, will find the first treatment the worst. This pain is not hurt-so-good pain; it is just painful. It took a while for the chronic spasms to get so bad, so it will take time before the person is clear of trigger points. If the person is very sensitive, go over the area lightly the next day. It may be two days or more before the person can handle another treatment, but each session gets easier and the person is encouraged by finally having relief from pain and gaining hope for complete relief. The pressure you use will vary in different areas of the body, from very much in the gluteals to very little on the face. If the painful muscle does not release the spasm, press a little harder. If the person can't take the pain, use less pressure.

The most common pain is the headache. It is estimated that forty million people in the United States suffer from chronic headaches. Thirty million pounds of aspirin are swallowed by headache sufferers to relieve the pain, which can originate from being overly tired or stressed, from an allergy, pollutants in the air, anxiety, anger, depression, a brain tumor, muscle spasms, or dental problems. The great majority of headaches are harmless, but they can make life miserable. I will briefly discuss three types of headaches: (1) muscle spasm or tension headaches; (2) temporomandibular joint dysfunction headaches; and (3) migraines.

1. The next time you walk down a street, observe the faces of people who walk by. You will see muscle tension written in their neck muscles, foreheads, and jaws. Muscle contraction is a sign of the stress of our times. This muscle tension can become a series of trigger points in the shoulder muscles, which refer pain to the head, to trigger points in the forehead, around the eyes, and in the masticator muscles of the jaw. Remember, an individual under stress is prepared for action by the "fight or flight" response, which consists of an automatic, instinctive bracing of skeletal muscles. Muscle spasms often occur in the neck, shoulders, forehead, around the ears, in the area between the shoulder blades, and around the spinal column.

If you have a stiff neck, examine the sore muscle and you will find trigger points that are very sore. Push with a finger to the count of seven and then release the pressure. It will hurt, but that is how the spasm is released. Then stretch your neck and roll your head in a circle.

Muscle spasm headaches are often caused by emotional stress and exhaustion that keep the muscles tense. Sometimes this is due to the nature of one's work. For example, I doubt if there is a court recorder without muscle spasms since the nature of the work requires the individual to be in a rigid position for long periods of time.

2. There is another type of headache that is often misdiagnosed or is not even recognized—a temporomandibular joint (TMJ) disorder, which causes head, neck, facial, and back pain. A TMJ disorder is basically a muscle spasm problem that produces chronic pain. There is very often limited movement of the jaw.

The temporomandibular joint, the jaw joint, is perhaps the most active joint in the body. It is the hinge at the side of the face that connects the jaw, or mandible, to the temporal bone of the skull. It moves every time the mouth opens and closes. This joint can be out of place as the result of a birth defect, a blow to the jaw, constant clenching of the teeth, poor posture, grinding the teeth at night, or opening the jaw too wide.

About 85 percent of sufferers of TMJ disorders have too much stress in their lives, which results in muscle spasms and secondary irritation of the joint. Conditions such as improperly fitting teeth, bad bite, and faulty nutrition can be the predisposing factors for TMJ muscle spasms and pain.

Symptoms of TMJ disorders range from pain in the jaw joints to intense headaches for which no pain medicine brings relief. The intense TMJ headache can be on one or both sides of the head and in the neck. As the muscle spasms create more trigger points, a person begins to favor the areas of pain by limiting the movement in those areas. Unfortunately, this only creates more imbalance of muscles and more spasms and triggers more pain, spreading down the neck to the shoulders, back, and even into the legs. A chronic TMJ disorder can eventually lead to curvature of the spine (scoliosis).

Other symptoms of TMJ disorders are a clicking, cracking, or grating sound when the mouth is opened or closed, dizziness, clogged sinuses, chronic sore throats, and earaches. There is often a ringing in the ears or a whooshing sound.

Generally speaking, dentists have favored the theory that the TMJ syndrome is caused by an improper alignment of teeth and jaws called malocclusion. To relieve the TMJ pain, it is necessary to correct the misalignment, properly repositioning the jaw, thus causing built-up muscle spasm tension to be relieved.

Dentists know that correcting the bite is not a complicated procedure. An acrylic appliance is made for the upper or lower teeth to help the muscles relax. Now, doesn't that sound simple? But dentists who use only a mechanical approach to solve the TMJ syndrome are perplexed when they see patients who have an improper alignment of the teeth and jaws, but have no pain! Equally perplexing are the patients who have a basically good alignment of teeth and jaws, but suffer from chronic TMJ pain.

To give you an example of the variables and complexities of TMJ disorders that must be examined, I'll describe what happened when a very fine dentist consulted me about a woman he was treating. This dentist knew I had been lecturing in dentistry since 1965. He had spent a great deal of money and time in continuing education in dentistry. He was very concerned and puzzled about this patient he had been treating for painful headaches due to malocclusion of her teeth, resulting in TMJ syndrome pains. He had been treating her with a night guard in her mouth to relieve the muscle tension during sleep, but to no avail.

During my conversation with the dentist, he told me that the woman's husband had recently asked him a very strange question, "How does high altitude relieve TMJ pain?" The dentist was a little startled and inquired why he would ask such a question. The husband's reply was that he had taken his family to Lake Tahoe for a two-week vacation, and during that time, his wife was free of her painful headaches. As soon as they returned to the lower altitude of Stockton, California, where they lived, the pain immediately attacked her again. When I heard this, I asked the dentist for more information.

"How long has she had the TMJ headaches?"

"For a year and a half."

"What is her occupation?"

"A telephone operator, but she has been on leave from her job and is on disability because of her headaches."

"How many children does she have, and what are their ages?"

"Three children, aged two, four, and six." (Now those are three good stress activators for any mother!)

"What is the size of their home?"

"Small."

"What changes have taken place in the family in the last year and half to two years?"

"The husband's mother moved in with them."

"Anything else happen recently in the family?"

"The wife is studying to become a Jehovah's Witness." (Now, the wife's becoming a Jehovah's Witness in a Roman Catholic family has serious ramifications. Within the theology of the Jehovah's Witness religion is the belief that the pope of the Roman Catholic church is the Antichrist. Naturally, Roman Catholics are very uncomfortable with this belief.)

It was evident that the wife's freedom from pain was due to her enjoyment of the two-week vacation at beautiful Lake Tahoe in a relaxed atmosphere. Returning to the valley and the constant stress of her home life triggered the muscle spasms that caused her TMJ pain.

The treatment of the TMJ syndrome is often very complex, involving many factors of stress, emotions, nutrition, body chemistry, relationship problems, and structural problems. I would caution a person about selecting any irreversible treatments such as grinding the teeth for occlusal adjustment or surgery of the TMJ joint.

3. The migraine headache is a vascular headache. Somehow there is malfunction in the mechanism for controlling changes in the diameters of the blood vessels of the head. A stimulus may cause an overconstriction of the vessels to the head and cause a reduced blood supply to various areas of the brain, resulting in symptoms of flashing lights, blurred vision or partial or total loss of vision for a while, a hypersensitivity to light, and a numbness or paralysis of a part of the body. Nausea and vomiting may also occur. The terrible pain can be overwhelming enough keep a person in bed, sometimes suffering for days or even weeks.

Emotional stress, repressed emotions, and emotional conflict can trigger migraine headaches, and so can chemicals in certain foods. Tyramine is a food chemical that dilates blood vessels and may induce headaches. Tyramine-high foods to avoid include the following:

- *Alcoholic beverages:* red wine especially; beer; ale; champagne; sherry; Riesling; sauterne.
- *Dairy products:* aged cheese like Roquefort; blue; Brie; Camembert; Gruyère, Cheddar.
- *Fish and meats:* salted dried fish like whitefish; pickled herring; sausages; beef liver and chicken liver; bologna; pepperoni; salami; summer sausage.
- *Vegetables:* avocados; Italian fava beans; sauerkraut.

- *Other:* chocolate, yeast; vanilla; soy sauce.
- *Monosodium glutamate:* found in Chinese foods; canned soups; seasoned salts; etc.
- *Nitrates:* found in hot dogs, turkey and chicken dogs; bacon.

The following foods have been known to produce headaches: milk chocolate, wheat, eggs, corn, peanuts, citrus fruits, pork, excessive refined sugar, and caffeine.

Birth control pills and menstruation often trigger migraines in women.

The migraine sufferer needs to find a physician who realizes that there are many triggers to a migraine and who will also be able to offer the medication that can help eliminate the headache.

Back pain alone accounts for more than eighteen million office visits per year to physicians. Dr. C. Norman Shealy wrote in *The Pain Game* that he strongly believes there are far too many operations for low back pain, particularly when it is caused by the pressure of a bulging or degenerative disc on a nerve rather than by a disc that has actually ruptured. Shealy reports that up to 40 percent of patients undergoing this back surgery fail to get relief and often the surgery itself can cause scar tissue that only increases the pain.[6]

By the time a person is past forty years of age, arthritis and bad discs will appear on X rays. Sometimes a disc is the root of the problem; in rare cases a ruptured or herniated disc may exert pressure on the nerves causing severe pain in the back, referring the pain all the way to the toes. However, at the Institute of Rehabilitation, New York University, Bellevue Medical Center, the doctors report that so many bad discs have been found in postmortems done on people who never complained of back pain that the damaged disc can hardly be called the main villain.

Specialist Dr. Paul Magnuson of Washington, D.C., said, "I've only seen one ruptured disc out of every thousand so diagnosed in over forty years of working on backs. Once upon a time everyone had sacroiliac trouble. Before that it was 'lumbago,' but now it's 'discs.'"[7]

Bonnie Prudden believes the real villain isn't discs but a combination of these conditions: (1) chronic muscle deficiency from lack of exercise, (2) chronic strain due to poor musculature, and (3) chronic pain due to trigger points causing the inadequate muscles to go into spasm.[8]

A person with chronic pain most likely will not improve until he is willing to assume personal responsibility for getting better and living with pain differently. Chronic pain often brings with it the decision of hopeless resignation to a life of misery and to the blackness of depression, especially when the person in pain goes from doctor to doctor in search of relief and still finds no answers, other than medication for pain. By then, the chronic pain sufferer knows that pain medication doesn't relieve the pain but brings another problem—addiction to pain medication and alcohol. Depression is a decision to fall into helplessness and hopelessness and give up personal responsibility. Then the chronic pain sufferer becomes convinced that nothing can be done to correct the source of pain, so the pain must be accepted on these hopeless terms. The longer the chronic pain, the greater the depression.

It is difficult but critical for the individual to realize the negative effects of focusing on the pain, being resigned to the pain, with the accompanying feelings of helplessness and hopelessness. This person must be willing to change his attitude, to accept the responsibility of achieving relief from the pain, agreeing not to talk about it. He must examine ways to change his reaction to the pain, to exercise, and to begin living as normal a life as possible.

The person must learn to deal with and verbalize the negative emotions of frustration, hostility, fear, guilt, resentment, and self-pity. Very often there is a real need to forgive those who have hurt the person and release all grudges to God for not healing him.

Dr. Shealy states that over time a "pain game" develops, which is an expensive and emotionally debilitating experience both for the person in pain and his family, with a bitter disappointment in the medical profession. There is no fun in this game. It is learned behavior. As long as the person allows his suffering to govern his behavior, there is little chance for relief, with no winners. This game must be broken up.

Pain is seen as more than just a hurt because for too many it is a life-style. Pain as a symptom says there is a serious disturbance in the body. Shealy says, "It is the reaction to pain, however, that determines whether the symptom has become a habit."[9]

It is very important to find out how family members react to the person with chronic pain. If pain is rewarded with attention, it becomes reinforced. If family members give attention to the person when he is active and not dwelling on sickness and pain, the pain game needn't start.

A person who had chronic pain came to see me. She had worn out several physicians and psychiatrists by her determination to remain miserable. People do have a right to be miserable, and some work very hard at it. My first instruction to her was to "shut up" and not talk about the pain and physical complaints at home for one week and see if she didn't feel better. I noticed a hopeful smile creep across her husband's face when I gave her those instructions. I assured her that she would be surprised by how much better she would feel and how much happier her husband would be. Sure enough, the next week she walked into the office with a positive attitude and strong posture and sat down and reported that she felt better than she had in years. Her husband agreed.

After telling me how good she felt, though, she suddenly realized that she had given up something very important to her; she was losing her role as a sick person with its power in secondary gains. Instantly she changed her positive body position and her confident voice to a whining "poor little me" tone again and said, "But, doctor, I don't think this will really work because I have all these problems. . . ."

Disability compensation rewards people for pain. In a sense, they cannot afford *not* to have pain, especially if it costs them income or if there is a lawsuit pending. Secondary gains from pain can have a disastrous effect on a marriage. The individual hurts too much to work, to enjoy a sexual relationship, to participate in leisure time activities, which would take the attention off pain. The person seeks attention by complaining, moaning, whining, limping, and being very dependent on the spouse. The resultant guilt and self-punishment create yet another powerful reinforcer for pain.

Neal Olshan writes about the six laws of pain behavior:

1. Don't talk about your pain!
2. Don't use pain as an excuse!
3. Don't use pain to get out of your responsibilities!
4. Don't let anyone become a professional nurse to you!
5. Don't use pain to manipulate others!
6. Don't be helpless/hopeless—always be positive![10]

Carl Simonton says the fear of pain for people with cancer is often the most frightening aspect of the disease. Every ache and pain has a new meaning.[11]

We have overreacted to symptoms of pain, and many of us are phobic about it. Could it be that we have, through television, become so terrified of pain that we believe we must always have painkillers on hand to quickly numb such feelings? The next evening you are watching television, just count all the commercials about relief from pain.

It would be wise for a person with the symptom of pain to think for a minute about what the pain is trying to communicate to him about his body and emotional life. Is the pain the result of abusing his body with too much stress, poor nutrition, poor sleeping habits, excessive eating, or too much alcohol? Are boredom and negative mental tapes doing their destructive work emotionally as well as physically? Before a person rushes to numb the pain with a pill, perhaps he should listen to what the pain is trying to say about what is out of balance in his life.

NOTES

1. Matt Clark, Marianna Gosnell, and Dan Shapiro, "The New War on Pain," *Newsweek*, April 25, 1977.
2. Norman Cousins, *Anatomy of an Illness* (New York: Bantam, 1981).
3. Bonnie Prudden, *Pain Erasure, the Bonnie Prudden Way* (New York: M. Evans & Co., 1980).
4. Neal H. Olshan, *Power Over Your Pain Without Drugs* (New York: Rawson, Wade, 1980).
5. Prudden, Ibid.
6. C. Norman Shealy, *The Pain Game* (Milbrae, Calif.: Celestian Arts, 1976).
7. Prudden, Ibid.
8. Ibid.
9. Shealy, Ibid.
10. Olshan, Ibid.
11. O. Carl Simonton, Stephanie Matthews-Simonton, and James L. Creighton, *Getting Well Again* (New York: Bantam, 1978).

CHAPTER SIX

EMOTIONS AND YOUR HEALTH

If the walls of my office could speak, they would tell stories of pain from the wounded who come seeking healing for their hurts. They would recall those who spoke of memories of . . .

Images of fear. Trying to be invisible and not make waves so my drunken daddy won't scream at me and hit me in the face. An image of fearfully cowering in the corner while cursing words of criticism, ridicule, and rejection tear at my heart.

"You're so stupid! Can't you do anything right?"

"You're an abomination of God!"

"I curse the day you were conceived."

Images of beatings while Mama screams, "You're bad. You're bad. I love you. Don't cry!" Mamma's eyes are wild with a fire of rage. Finally her arms are so tired she can't hit any more. "Mamma, why do you hate me so? Am I a bad seed that must be destroyed?"

Images of the night and its fears. Hearing my parents fight—words of hate, screams of pain, sounds of things being smashed. They're trying to kill each other! Is it my fault they fight? Fear of the nights when my father comes to my bedroom to sexually use and abuse me—afraid to tell. The pain is so awful. I feel so dirty . . . so guilty . . . but why?

All this pain. What shall I do with my pain? Deny it? Suppress it? Try to forget it? I'll hide it behind the stone walls in the cellar of my mind, these memories of hurts too painful to remember.

The tears—too many tears. I'll never cry again. Pools of pain bottled up inside. Pools of water, drunk with despair. If I cried, who would care?

It's not fair!

God, where are You? Why me?

Do You hate me, too?

I only wanted to be loved.

I need love, but I'm afraid to love.

I can't risk rejection again.

I am angry—so angry from all my hurts.

It is more than anger now. It is a burning fire of rage that's been fed from an early age.

I have so much anger and violence inside, if I'm not careful, I could kill.

Take another pill—another drink. I'm so close to the edge, the brink of murder, suicide, and death.

Death could bring the peace I haven't found in life.

A life of pain, rejection, bitterness, and hate. It's no wonder that I'm sick.

The more I work as a psychotherapist, the more I am overwhelmed by the amount and the intensity of emotional pain and deep woundedness in people's lives. These people are not psychotic or neurotic, just humans who have sustained injuries that can't be helped by Band-Aids. Giving wounded people diagnostic labels and putting them in neat, scientific categories only hurts them more.

The wounds are not healed by medication to treat the symptoms and numb the pain. To set up a schedule of behavior modification to reward or extinguish specific behavioral responses doesn't heal the deep woundedness. I have also realized for a long time that uncovering the deep woundedness in therapy may not always produce the healing that is needed. A man once said to me in therapy, "I never realized before how much my father hated me and hurt me, so now that I know, what do I do with this information?"

Through psychotherapy, uncovering the woundedness and talking about it can bring only so much relief. In fact, some people are better off without recalling their pain if there is not, in addition to the insights, a healing of the past.

Intense emotional pain is very often the soil from which develops physical illness in a person's life. Often the deep emotion of woundedness begins in the womb. Thomas Verny, M.D., in his book *The Secret Life of the Unborn Child,* writes from research conducted in prenatal clinics in Europe and the United States that "the unborn child is a feeling, remembering, aware being, and because he is, what happens to him—what happens to all of us—in the nine months between conception and birth, molds and shapes our personality, drives, and ambitions in very important ways."[1]

We have known that a pregnant woman who drinks alcohol and smokes cigarettes can damage the child in the womb, but if the mother listens to rock and roll music or hard rock, that baby will be very nervous and jumpy compared to a baby whose mother listened to soothing music and who will most likely be calm.

One of the most important influences on the baby in the womb, especially from six months to birth, is the kind of emotions communicated from the mother, the father, and other significant people around the mother. Ongoing negative emotions are capable of deeply wounding the child within. What the expectant mother feels and verbalizes makes a difference in what the child experiences in the womb: words and emotions of being loved, wanted or not wanted, being threatened with abortion, and even the sex preferences of the parents. For example, if the parents keep talking about their "little boy" but their "little boy" is a girl, this can create problems regarding the girl's sexuality and her awareness of being a disappointment to her parents because she is not a male.

There is also a physiological means of communicating anger and fear to the baby in the womb. Under stress, the mother releases from her adrenals the "fight" or "flight" hormones of anger or fear. These hormones enter the mother's blood and pass through the placental barrier, causing the baby to experience anger and fear. If the stress is chronic, it can cause a spontaneous abortion.

A few years ago I worked with a young woman for her emotional problems of fear and depression. She and her newly married husband were living with his brother and wife. They had just gone to bed after watching a late movie, *From Here to Eternity*. At approximately 12:30 A.M. something exploded in their bedroom; the woman jumped out of bed to get out of the bedroom, but the door wouldn't open because of the rubble of broken cement blocks. Her brother-in-law shoved the door open, and through the wall where the headboard of the bed had been were now the headlights of an automobile driven by a drunk who had missed the curve in front of the house.

The husband and wife were terrified and suffered from some cuts and bruises, but when they went to a hospital emergency room, they discovered that the husband had forgotten to bring his hospitalization card along. So they went to the county hospital where they waited for a couple of hours. When no one took care of them, they went home disgusted and still cut and bruised.

The house creaked and groaned at night after the accident and every time a car went around the curve, they were fearful of its hitting the house. To protect themselves, they parked their cars in positions to protect the house. One day the woman walked out the front door just in time to see a motorcyclist miss the curve and hit the house exactly where the drunk had hit it.

Shortly thereafter she went to the doctor for a heavy flow of blood, which turned out to be a miscarriage. This was in April. In September the woman had another miscarriage. Finally, a year later, she was able to give birth to a little girl, but she spent most of the pregnancy in bed for fear of falling and anxiety over a miscarriage. Because of the chronic stress of fear, the couple decided to have only one child.

I now appreciate more fully the account of Mary's visit to Elizabeth when she told her the glorious news of the visitation by the angel Gabriel who announced that she would give birth to the Messiah. "And it happened, when Elizabeth heard the greeting of Mary, that the babe leaped in her womb; and Elizabeth was filled with the Holy Spirit" (Luke 1:41); in the womb the baby John responded to his mother's excitement and joy.

What can expectant parents do to help the baby in the womb to be healthy and develop good self-esteem? The expectant mother can help the life of the unborn child by not smoking, not drinking alcohol, not drinking liquids with caffeine, avoiding chronic stress, and staying away from toxic substances such as pesticides. She should eat a balanced diet, take vitamin and mineral supplements, and take time to relax to restful music.

From six months on, the expectant mother and father can put their hands on the abdomen and tell the child within how much they already love the child and how happy they will be when they can hold and love the baby after birth. I asked our daughter, Jan, and her husband, Scott, to live with us while he finished his college education. Ever since Jan was a little girl, she had wanted to be a mother. So when Jan became pregnant, she and Scott did all the positive, loving, healthy things for the child within the womb. When Courtney was born, she already knew she was loved with unconditional love. As grandparents, we also have the joy of loving her in our home. As I write this, Courtney is eight months old, has never been sick, and is a very calm, happy, loving baby. I just wish my other five grandchildren were living closer because I love being a grandfather.

I firmly believe that the greatest gift parents can give a child is unconditional love expressed in lots of hugs and words, daily repeated, especially at bedtime: "I love you for being you. I'm the most blessed parent in the world to have a child like you. I thank God that I have you as my son (or daughter)." Then hug the child and put the child to bed.

Unfortunately, too many people were rejected, not wanted, when they were in the womb. This rejection is the root of depression in later life. In working with an individual in therapy, I always inquire about any knowledge the person may have about what was going on in the parents' lives when the person was conceived. I ask if the parents were having problems in their marriage, if the pregnancy was unwanted or unexpected. Did the parents have to get married because of the pregnancy? Were the parents expecting a boy or girl and the individual disappointed them?

It is amazing how much people have heard from their parents or relatives about the time they were in the womb. Here are a few remarks that have been reported to me.

"I curse the day you were conceived."

"My mother tried to abort me by falling down the stairs."

"My mom and dad were so excited about the pregnancy that they held a party for their friends and family to announce the good news. The day of the party my mother's mom died unexpectedly, and my mom was deeply depressed for a long time."

"I was being born by natural means when all of a sudden the doctor had to perform surgery to deliver me. As I was being lifted out, my mother had a seizure, vomited, and some of the vomit went into the abdomen. The doctor's green outfit was soaked with blood when he told my father he doubted if he could save the life of his wife. My mom was in bed very sick for months after I was born."

The deep hurts of rejection during the vulnerable months in the womb and in early childhood have a devastating effect on a person's self-esteem and emotional, mental, spiritual, and physical well-being.

Children are helpless and defenseless against the cruel, hurtful words that they may receive from their parents. To children, parents are all-knowing and powerful, like God. When a child has an angry, abusive father, it is not surprising that the child has a tendency to reject or fear God as heavenly Father.

Children are very sensitive, keen observers of the world in which they live, but because they have insufficient life experience, they can make very poor interpretations and conclusions about what they observe. A young child does not understand that his parents have problems and they are the troubled ones. A child does not know that the parents' problems exist apart from him. When the parents have chronic, severe problems in their relationship that they cannot resolve, a child has difficulty interpreting his world accurately, especially when the parents choose to make him the scapegoat of their problems and unhappiness.

The scapegoated child is placed in a double-bind situation. Somehow his parents' unhappiness is all his fault, and no matter how hard he tries to please them—to be loved—the more he experiences rejection and guilt and is driven deeper into the blackness of rejection and depression, making it almost impossible to escape. The woundedness may bring rebellion, acting out behavior, and problems in school, then perhaps trouble with the law or drug use to ease the suffering. It may bring sleep troubled by nightmares that won't quit and won't go away with the dawn of a new day.

I have worked with many foster children and adopted children who experienced the deep pain of rejection while they were in the womb and the reality that their mothers did not want them, so they were handed over to foster parents, placed in orphanages, or given to adoptive parents.

A child who has been given away by the birth mother suffers a deep hurt from rejection that causes "a certain funny feeling deep inside that I'm not okay." A child will try to find something he has done wrong that is causing him to feel bad. Then there comes the sinking feeling in the pit of the stomach that "I have done nothing bad, so maybe when I was born my mother knew I was a 'bad seed' and got rid of me."

This deep wound can produce either the overcompliant child who compulsively strives to please and gain approval from the world or the child who erupts with rage and rebellion at puberty. The adoptive mother is overwhelmed by the sudden fury of rage directed at her. The good student becomes the failing, marginal student. There are lots of family arguments, episodes of running away, trouble with the law, and parents searching for help for the young person they adopted.

In trying to help a child who was given away by the birth mother, I have tried to dislodge the fixed idea of being a bad seed. I try to have the young person look at the whole process differently by suggesting that the birth mother had real problems and her decision to give up her child was made out of the pain of her love for her child and her wish to give the child a better chance in life, a chance to have two parents who would love and provide for the baby, far better than the mother alone could promise.

There is a special pain experienced by the foster child who is shifted from home to home, often physically and sexually abused. It is a life of repeated rejection and loneliness and little, if any, love. I asked an eighteen-year-old girl who was coming to group therapy for the first time at Napa State Hospital her name, and she replied, "My name is Raggedy Ann. I have been to thirty-eight foster homes, and I don't want to make a permanent home in the state hospital. I'm the kid with ugly fitting dresses and cloppy shoes at least two sizes too big, always teased and laughed at by other kids at school. No one has ever loved me or wanted me." Years later I wrote this poem about "Raggedy Ann."

The Welfare Child

Am I just an orphan, a ward or a case?
A problem to be solved?
All I want is a permanent place
To feel wanted and loved.
Really, I'm not wild.
I'm just a welfare child.
No one saw my tears
Or cared that I was blue.
I just wanted to be like you
With a loving mom and dad
And a home.
But all I do is wander and roam.
Where do I belong? became my lonely song.
I've done no terrible wrong.
Please, won't somebody love me?
Take me just as I am?
Not as a welfare child
But as a child of God.
I'm tired of sharing beds,
Lice in my head, beans, and bread.
Another school makes me so ill at ease
New kids who cruelly tease—
"There's Raggedy Ann with hand-me-down
Clothes and those clippity cloppy shoes."
No one sees my tears
Or feels my painful fears.
Nobody cares that I'm here.

The experiences of rejection and the fear of rejection create a poor self-image and a defensiveness in trusting another person, an inability to accept love. The individual has such a basic lack of self-love and acceptance that these thoughts become common: *If I can't love myself and believe I am worth loving, why should I believe that anyone else could love me? If I reveal myself to you, you wouldn't love me. You would probably laugh or throw up or reject me . . . or all three.*

Fear of rejection often sets in motion a self-fulfilling prophecy of setting oneself up for rejection again and again. A person who is troubled with jealousy has serious self-doubts about trusting herself: *If I can't trust myself, why should I trust you? I will trust you only as long as I can control you.* The self-doubt is transferred to the other person and often drives the other person away, proving that the other person would reject her.

If a person is to be emotionally healthy, the wounded memories and emotions need healing. I have searched for the means to heal the deep woundedness, and since 1981, I have used psychotherapy plus the Holy Spirit for inner healing. I am simply a conduit for the Holy Spirit to flow through me as I anoint with oil and lay my left hand on a person's head and pray for the anointing of the Holy Spirit so the deep hurts and wounds in the memories and emotions can be healed. I cannot heal wounds of rejection from the time a person was in the womb, but the Holy Spirit can and does heal those wounds. I have often noticed that as the Holy Spirit is healing the emotional and mental hurts, there is a corresponding physical healing—a person with seriously high blood pressure becomes normal, or a person with chronic pain is healed of that pain.

It has taken a long time for medical science to realize that a person's emotions can have such powerful (and sometimes hazardous) effects on health. As far back as the second century A.D., the Greek physician Galen observed that depressed women were more prone to breast cancer than their cheerful counterparts. A century ago Sir Jean Paget wrote this about cancer: "The causes are so frequent in which there is deep anxiety, deferred hope and disappointment, quickly followed by the growth and increase of cancer that we can hardly doubt that mental depression is a weighty additive to the other influences favoring the development of the cancerous condition."

There have been these insights into the relationship of emotions and illness for thousands of years, yet they have been slow to be investigated and accepted by the medical profession. In the 1920s when Dr. Smith Ely Jeliffe spoke before the New York Academy of Medicine about the concept that emotional and mental disturbances can create physical illness, his professional peers laughed at him and suggested that he join the Christian Science church. Dr. Jeliffe was so hurt emotionally by the ridicule and mocking that he died a short time after the meeting of a broken heart.[2]

The term *psychosomatic* was too often used to imply that since there was no organic basis for a person's symptoms, it was "all in the head," meaning the illness was imaginary and did not really exist. Carlton Fredericks writes, "This is tragically illustrated in the history of a group of more than one hundred patients whose complaints had been dismissed as 'psychosomatic,' more than twenty-five of whom subsequently died of cancer." Examination of every one of the other patients revealed the presence of physical diseases that were responsible for the psychosomatic symptoms.[3]

In the last few years a brand-new scientific field called psychoneuroimmunology has developed. This field is based on the belief that the body's immune system can be affected emotionally and mentally to increase or decrease disease susceptibility. Finally, medical science and psychology are developing a more comprehensive view of how our emotional lives directly affect our physical well-being by investigating the actual links between psychological events, brain function, hormone secretion, and the potency of the immune response.[4]

A wealth of evidence has been gathered to show that the single most important predictor of cancer is the death of a spouse or other significant person, like a child, or a devastating divorce in the past one or two years. There is a lower production of T cells in the subsequent weeks and months that can last up to a year in the grieving person. In only one day traumatic shock can lower the number of the healing warriors in the immune system.

I believe that some divorces may be even more destructive to the health of the divorcées than the death of a partner because of the hateful wounds inflicted during the situation. When there are children, the relationship often must continue for many years, thus delaying the healing of all the wounds.

James J. Lynch reports in *The Broken Heart* that almost every type of cancer is significantly influenced by marital status, with widowed, divorced, and single individuals almost always having signficantly higher death rates than married persons. For divorced, widowed, and single men, the overall death rates from cardiovascular disease were two to three times higher than for married men. Similar trends were also true for women. For almost every other major cause of premature death, there were also marked increases for the nonmarried over the married, sometimes with differences in death rates as high as tenfold.[5]

Have you ever wondered why all the people who smoke cigarettes don't get lung cancer? It seems that the big determining factor is depression, which is known to suppress the production of killer T cells in the immune system, thus causing the lung cancer to develop.

Since the 1960s, psychologist Lawrence LeShan has been studying the psychological and emotional variables of people with cancer. For years his work was virtually ignored and viewed as suspect, but now the role of the emotional and mental aspects of people with cancer is widely accepted. LeShan states,

> I am a psychotherapist and not a medical researcher. But on the basis of my work with dozens of terminal cancer patients in intensive psychotherapy, as well as extensive study of the personality of hundreds of other cancer victims, there is a generalization that I believe can be made with great certainty: the presence of cancer is usually an indication that there is something else wrong in the life of the patient. The cancer victim usually has a psychological orientation that increases the chances of getting cancer and makes it more difficult for many individuals to fight for their lives when they do develop a malignancy.[6]

In his early research with cancer patients for causes or predisposing causes, LeShan found first that the loss of the central relationship in a person's life could be catastrophic, causing a loss of reasons for being. The loss of a crucial relationship, which had occurred in the lives of 72 percent of the patients, was the most significant clue in his search for possible real relationships between the life history of the individual and vulnerability to cancer.

The second most prevalent cause was the inability to express hostility in their own defense. These people could stand strongly and aggressively in defense of the rights of others, such as family members, or of ideas. But they generally were unable to express their own needs, wishes, and feelings.

In psychotherapy with cancer patients, LeShan found that often there was a poor self-image. The cancer patient had a lot of self-dislike and self-distrust, which prevent the building of open, trusting relationships with others. This naturally results in loneliness, unmet emotional needs, and a despair of life. The inner bitterness surfaces in relationships with people. Thus, when this person develops cancer, there is no real hope for life because when the person was well, there was no joy or hope in life. Why should it be any different now that the person has cancer? LeShan notes, "I have found that often this low self-image and despair of life person has subconsciously been waiting for cancer as a socially acceptable form of suicide."[7]

The research concerning the emotional and psychological makeup of people who have cancer paints a picture of repressed, self-denying individuals who have a low self-image, cannot express anger on their own behalf, have a history of cold, unsatisfying relationships with their parents, and have experienced a significant loss in relationships.

Everyone has stress to deal with in life, but the person who has cancer is overwhelmed and overreacts to the stressful events. This person feels the need to present a strong, positive image to the world, and he frequently denies negative feelings, leading him to feel that he cannot change the things that bother him. Thus, he perceives himself as a victim who must suffer in silence without admitting the negative emotions and fears to anyone. He simply "bites the bullet" and suffers.

Boris Pasternak wrote in *Doctor Zhivago,*

> The great majority of us are required to live a life of constant, systematic duplicity. Your health is bound to be affected if, day after day, you say the opposite of what you feel, if you grovel before what you dislike and rejoice at what brings you nothing but misfortune. Our nervous system isn't just a fiction, it's part of our physical body, and our soul exists in space and is inside us, like the teeth in our mouth. It can't be forever violated with impunity.

Depression comes in many forms. Depression is a decision to surrender to hopelessness and helplessness. The depressed person gives up responsibility for his life and healing. Life is acted out in slow motion. Everything is too much effort. Life is dull and boring, and there is no motivation or ambition. Friends, family, and physicians can offer a thousand helpful solutions but the depressed person usually responds, "Yes but— that won't work for me."

Once I was working with a fifty-seven-year-old man who had been fired from his job as the vice president of sales. He had never been fired before, and he had always been successful. He became so depressed that he was suicidal. I confronted him with his decision to surrender to the hopelessness and helplessness, and told him that since it was his decision, he had a right to be miserable and depressed. Nothing or no one could help him until he took responsibility for getting well. He admitted that he had given in to the hopelessness and helplessness, and then asked me, "You mean that you don't have a 'magic pill' for me?" I told him that I had no magic pill, but he could make a decision of hope, to believe in himself again, and take personal responsibility for his life and his healing. Then he would be on the path out of the darkness of depression and headed toward the light of a new day.

Another form of depression is anger that has been turned inward. The person has been programmed not to express anger and has had no permission to express his anger and hurts in his own defense. The inability to express anger may also result in physical symptoms, such as bottled-up anger locked in the joints in bones or in persistent headaches. This type of depression can be difficult to help in therapy because so often the source of hurt and anger is blocked by denial.

Guilt can produce another form of depression. You can feel guilty from violating your moral and spiritual values. The importance of guilt lies in giving you a message that you have done something wrong, which creates a tension that becomes a strong stimulus to rectify the wrong, or at least ask forgiveness of the person wronged. Even though it is painful to your pride to go to a wronged party and ask forgiveness, the very act of confession is beneficial to you because it allows the discharge of the negative, destructive energy of guilt. The act of confession is also healthful for the person who has been hurt, because in the granting of forgiveness, the healing of the hurt can be completed. Forgiveness is the eraser that wipes the slate clean.

Another form of depression is due to a physiological basis, from a lack of the trace mineral lithium. This deficiency is believed to be hereditary in nature; the genetic basis is usually from the father's side of the family. This form of depression is called manic-depressive or bipolar disorder. The mood swings can go to an extreme high of great activity and well-being to an extreme low of depression. Everyone has emotional highs and lows, but with the bipolar or manic-depressive, the mood swings are extreme. Treatment with the trace mineral lithium is often helpful in stabilizing the mood swings.

Depression is also being treated as a chemical imbalance in the serotonin fluid in the brain, and physicians and psychiatrists currently prescribe medication for depression. Medical science is conducting major research into brain chemistry and mental illness. Research is promising, and researchers are hopeful we will know more about treating the biochemical basis for depression in the near future.

Depression is not only a serious emotional problem, but it is disruptive to the natural healing powers of the stress response and the immune system.

Thomas Holmes, a Seattle psychiatrist, studied how an emotion, such as depression, can affect a person with a germ-related illness, such as tuberculosis. Inflammation is the reaction of living tissue to invasion by a germ. The stress response is to send cortisone from the adrenal glands to combat the inflammation. The level of cortisone in the blood to fight the TB germs varied with the patient's emotional state. As long as the patient felt hopeless, depressed, withdrawn, apathetic, and overwhelmed, he had very little resistance, and the tuberculosis did not improve, even with high doses of antibiotics. If the patient's mood of depression improved, the adrenal glands released more cortisone, which enabled the antibiotic to be effective in healing the tuberculosis.

Dr. Holmes theorizes that when the amount of life changes, which trigger the stress response, become overwhelming, the person simply gives up and falls into the hopelessness and helplessness of depression. The brain, Holmes postulates, turns off the adrenal cortex, which stops producing the protective hormones. Then the germ, if present, can do its destructive work.[8]

The best way to handle the effect of depression and trauma from the death of a loved one is to develop a healthy theology of suffering and death. How to deal with grief is a subject that is seldom spoken of until we are in the midst of a grief experience. Death always seems to come as a shock, even though we consciously know and rationalize that it is the other side of the coin of life. Pain and death are facts of life. We sometimes forget that we are not going to get out of this thing alive. How much better off we would be if we made peace with death at twenty-one, so we wouldn't have to spend the rest of our life worrying about it.

Some Christians believe they are given at birth a comprehensive insurance policy from "Lord and Son" that will protect them from pain, sickness, accident, and death. Thus, when a tragedy happens to a Christian, people say with a puzzled voice, "But he or she was such a good Christian." Life is not fair and that is fact! The beginning of wisdom is that when you try to make sense of suffering and life, you go nuts—unless you have a healthy belief in God, suffering, and death.

Sheldon Kopp, who was suffering from a brain tumor when he wrote *If You Meet the Buddha on the Road, Kill Him!*, says,

Much suffering results from an erroneous outlook on life. In one way or another a person has acquired a picture of his place in life which simply isn't true. Feeling helpless in the midst of conflict and suffering, he allows his life to be molded by circumstances until he feels himself to be little more than a victim of fate. Many people feel that they can accept their suffering in this ambiguous, imperfect, mixed bag of life, if only some guru can tell them why it should be this way. If there is some reason for their suffering, some explanation for their unhappiness, some purpose to their enduring the ups and downs of living, then it's a deal. Otherwise, they will hold out stubbornly, digging in their heels. They do not see that this results in doubling their grief by making them unhappy about being unhappy.[9]

As a Lutheran pastor, I have been involved in many tragic incidents with families when there was a death. My most difficult tasks in ministering to the family at a time of grief were not only in trying to help them come to terms with the grief reaction, but also in trying to undo the damage that was done by well-meaning friends and relatives as they tried in their simple way to give explanations and comfort as to why the loved one died. For instance, I often heard people say, "Well, cheer up, it's God's will," or "God wanted your son or daughter." In essence, they were saying that God caused the death.

When God is believed to be the cause of the death of a loved one, people can be filled with rage and bitterness toward Him. I have always been a fan of C. S. Lewis. After he wrote *The Problem of Pain,* in which he focused on the problem of suffering, his wife died. The problem of pain became very personal, and all his brilliant reasoning was of no value. He, like Job, wailed in anguish and anger against God for taking his wife. Later on he wrote a book on his grief, but he used a pseudonym. He finally admitted he was the author and called the book *A Grief Observed.* Listen to the pain and rage against God in his words:

But go to Him when your need is desperate, when all other help is vain, and what do you find? A door slammed in your face, and a sound of bolting and double bolting inside. After that, silence. You may as well turn away. The longer you wait, the more emphatic the silence will become.

Not that I am (I think) in much danger of ceasing to believe in God. The real danger is of coming to believe such dreadful things about Him. The conclusion I dread is not, "So there is no God after all," but "So this is what God's really like. Deceive yourself no longer."

There is no answer. Only the locked door, the iron curtain, the vacuum, absolute zero. "Them that asks, don't get." I was a fool to ask.[10]

There is a difference between God's willing or causing a death and God's allowing a death. The same factors occur when you buy roller skates for a child. You allow the child to have fun skating, but at the same time you accept the possibility that she might fall and get hurt. However, it's a little different when the child is skating and you suddenly stick out your foot and trip her. That's willing or causing your child to be hurt. Perhaps some people can accept a death better if they feel that God caused it, but God does not go around filling bodies with cancer or using drunks to kill families on the highway.

Jesus knew why He came to earth. He came to do the will of the Father who sent Him, and He did only what He saw the Father doing. At the synagogue in Nazareth, Jesus read these words:

> *The Spirit of the LORD is upon Me,*
> *Because He has anointed Me to*
> *   preach the gospel to the poor;*
> *He has sent Me to heal the brokenhearted,*
> *To proclaim liberty to captives*
> *And recovery of sight to the blind,*
> *To set at liberty those who are oppressed;*
> *To proclaim the acceptable year of the LORD (Luke 4:18–19).*

He closed the book, handed it back to the attendant in the synagogue, gazed at him intently, and then added, "Today this Scripture is fulfilled in your hearing" (Luke 4:20–21).

And Jesus did heal the brokenhearted, cast out demons, cure the sick, and raise the dead. In the death and resurrection of Jesus, God won a great victory over Satan and our mutual enemy—death: "For He must reign till He has put all enemies under His feet. The last enemy that will be destroyed is death" (1 Cor. 15:25–26).

Death, then, is not the handmaiden of God, but the enemy of God and man and will be destroyed. My faith is in the God who created life, who raised Christ from the dead, and who has promised us that same resurrection and victory over death. Instead of saying to a person that it was God's will, or that God took a loved one, I'd rather share with a person a God who knows what it is to grieve and love a Son, and to offer a Son to a very painful death on a cross that truly "wasn't fair."

I have often replied to the question, "Why did my loved one die?" by asking what the death certificate said as to the cause of death. Was it cancer, a coronary, or injuries from a car accident? These are the reasons for death. The fact of death is that we are vulnerable as humans.

In order for the grief process to be a healing process, it must be experienced emotionally. At first family members are in a state of shock from the death of a loved one. They are numb and unable to realize the emotional loss and trauma. Too often friends and relatives think the family members are handling their grief very well because they are not falling apart, but when that takes place, hopefully about three or four weeks later, no one may be present to be emotionally supportive.

I have used three weeks after the death of a loved one to minister to the grieving ones. I encourage the person, or persons, to express the tears and emotions that range from anger to fear to despair. I give people permission to cry and face whatever is there so they can, in time, finally say good-bye to the one who died.

Children are too often ignored or made to feel that they shouldn't be around mourning family members. The suppressed grief reaction in children will become depression, but they often display the depression by striking out at the world in angry, disruptive behavior. No one sees this behavior as depression. If the emotional grief in children is not dealt with, it can create real problems for them in learning how to react emotionally in adulthood.

A woman in therapy named Sue was having a difficult time expressing her emotions, especially anger. She and her husband were separated, and he was living in another state. I once asked her if she ever got angry with her husband. She thought for a while and said, "Oh, I got mad at him once when he had an affair with another woman. This woman had been our baby-sitter one night."

I interrupted and said, "Did you know that she was the 'other woman'?"

"Oh, yes," she replied.

I asked, "What made you mad that night?"

"Well, when she got in the car to be taken home by my husband, she asked me to get a blanket for her feet, so I went in the house for a blanket and brought it out to her. Then I saw my husband hand her a long-stemmed red rose. I was so mad I went upstairs and went to bed and fell asleep."

Now, I don't think that is a proper, healthy expression of anger. I asked, "Sue, how did you become so disconnected from your emotions? What happened to you as a little girl?"

She told of hearing her parents fight when she was very small and about how frightened that made her. "I remember now, when I was four, hearing a terrible fight between Mom and Dad. Dad was an alcoholic, and Mom was always furious with him for drinking. That night Dad was really drunk, and

Mom told him to leave the house. I was so scared, but I didn't know what to do. I looked at my brother who was seven and he showed no emotions, so maybe I decided that is how you handle emotions. I really loved my dad, but in two months or so my parents got a divorce and a couple of months later, my daddy died. I never got to see him alive again after he left the house that awful night. My mother destroyed all the pictures of him, so I could only see his picture at my aunt's home."

I asked, "When did you cry for your daddy's death?"

"When I was thirteen," she replied.

"Then you could face the fact that he was never coming home again?"

"Yes," she replied softly, and began to cry—a cry that lasted for three or four days.

I will often suggest to a person who has not said good-bye to a loved one who has died to write a letter saying how much that loved one is missed. One woman said that after her mother died when she was nine, she and her brothers stayed with her mom's mother. The grandmother was very upset by her daughter's death and would say to her grandchildren, "Don't ever forget your mother." When the father started dating and eventually married again, the grandmother was furious with him and told the grandchildren, "Your father should not have found another to try to take the place of your mother. Don't you ever forget your mother." As a result, the girl never could say good-bye to her mom until she was a grown woman; only then could she say good-bye without feeling guilty about it.

Emotions are energy, and energy that is not released or expressed goes inside the body to be locked in muscles, organs, or areas of physical weakness. When that energy is denied and suppressed, it retreats into the subconscious mind where it makes demands on your being. As John Powell said, "When I suppress an emotion, my stomach keeps score—one, two, three, four."[11] Repressed emotions of anger and fear have a 95 percent correlation rate with coronaries, cancer, and strokes.

One sign of the healing of deep emotional hurts is that when a person is getting better, the energy used to suppress and deny emotions is relaxed, then the frozen pain defrosts, the black depression is released, and the rage comes out. When this happens, the person is very surprised and confused because he is doing much better. Even though I warn that these emotions will emerge when he is feeling better, he forgets or doesn't believe how intense is the emotional energy when it is released. When this release takes place, a person will call me, and I will explain, "I told you it would hurt, but you didn't believe that it would hurt this much. Don't be discouraged because this is a healing process." The person is relieved, but still experiences the pain.

Have you been programmed to be emotionally constipated and never "make waves" or "rock the boat" or express the anger in your own defense? Emotions are expressions of how a person hurts. What you feel is neither good nor bad. It is what you are experiencing. Your reaction to the emotional hurt is your responsibility. That reaction can be harmful or helpful.

When you are hurt, anger results. If the anger is released in a healthy way, no damage is done. I have found it helpful to sleep on a hurt to gain control of the anger and gain a perspective on my hurt and anger so I do not overreact and explode, which may not be healthy or helpful. Then I can report my hurt to the person who maltreated me without lashing out in anger or turning the anger inward where it becomes depression. If I dwell on the hurt, I can easily become resentful, bitter, and finally filled with hate for the person who wronged me.

You and I are responsible for our emotional reactions. If we react to hurt with resentment, bitterness, or hate, then that is our responsibility and our sin, which must be confessed. We do not have to react that way. The Bible cautions, "[Look] carefully lest anyone fall short of the grace of God; lest any root of bitterness springing up cause trouble and by this many become defiled" (Heb. 12:15).

I define *hate* as the "means by which I punish and destroy myself for the actions of another." My hate does nothing to the person who hurt me, but it does destroy me. I figured out that if a person hurts me once, that is enough, and if I dwell on the hurt so it becomes hate, I am destroying myself.

Focusing on just releasing the pent-up anger by expressing all the anger may not be healing and can be harmful to your health, causing a coronary or a stroke. Lynn, a woman in her late twenties, was referred to me by her physician who called to see if I could see her right away. Lynn came into my office and said, "I'm so angry that I'm about to explode." She immediately began talking at a machine-gun rate, telling me she had been getting counseling for months to get out her anger. Her therapist had her pounding pillows, shouting, screaming, and running, which she hated, to get her anger out. The angrier she got, the higher her blood pressure went. To top it all off, Lynn said, "Last week while I was pounding my high-school baton on the kitchen floor, the end of the baton flew off and struck me in the right eye, giving me an ugly black eye. That did it! I asked my physician to recommend a different psychotherapist. He was very concerned that I might have a stroke or a coronary from this anger therapy."

I asked Lynn to relax in my reclining chair and tell about the hurts that had caused all her anger. Immediately, she began to tell about the hurt of her husband's leaving her and her life-long rejection by her family.

In the weeks that followed, the emotional pain that had been suppressed for so long began to be released. Lynn felt that the top of her head would explode. It was the "frozen pain" finally defrosting and demanding release. One evening she called me on the phone and said, "I'm getting close to tears." I had given her permission to cry, and the tears finally came. That cry lasted for three days.

If you don't deal with your anger, it will deal with you in a destructive way. In *Arthritis, Medicine, and the Spiritual Laws* Dr. Loring Swaim of Harvard Medical School wrote that his research found that the first attack of rheumatoid arthritis almost always followed traumatic, emotional events in patients' lives. Dr. Swaim also discovered that many arthritic patients had unresolved emotional conflicts behind their physical symptoms of disease. They all harbored feelings of resentment, unforgiveness, fear, or anger. When the patients would own up to their emotions of resentment and bitterness and forgive those who had hurt them and made them angry, and when they also forgave themselves, the active disease process of rheumatoid arthritis was frequently arrested. The disease would remain quiet until patients again failed to deal with anger or guilt. Forgiveness again made the attack subside.[12]

Forgiveness of others and self is a necessary step for healing and health. Forgiveness is the single most selfish thing I can do for myself. When I forgive someone, I get rid of the pain, and I don't like pain!

Joe and Ellen had been married for twenty years, and the marriage had been a painful one. They were ready to call it quits. After the first counseling session, Joe went to visit his parents. He had given up on the marriage. Ellen came in alone, and she was very dejected. She revealed that they were engaged to be married when Ellen discovered she was pregnant. Joe had talked to her parents and reassured them that he would take good care of their daughter and never leave her.

I asked Ellen if she could remember her emotional reaction to the news that she was pregnant. Ellen said, "Oh, yes, I can remember it just as though it was yesterday. I felt humiliated because we lived in a small midwestern town, and we were very active in church as a family. I felt dirty about being pregnant, and my husband was repulsive to me."

I asked Ellen if she had made an inner vow to herself about Joe when she found out she was pregnant. Ellen soon realized that she had an inner vow that said, "I will not give him pleasure or any love, and I will punish him for getting me pregnant." Ellen went on to say she was numb emotionally toward Joe until this inner vow was revealed. Ellen was shocked at what she discovered about herself and said, "For twenty years, Joe has tried and tried to make it up to me for getting me pregnant, and I have always rejected him. That's why he has given up and put all his energy and time into his work."

I asked Ellen to renounce her inner vow and confess to God her sin of the inner vow and her sins of bitterness, resentment, and hate. Then I asked her to forgive Joe for getting her pregnant and to forgive herself. Ellen did this, and I assured her that God forgave her. Ellen was ashamed of herself and said she hoped it was not too late for their marriage.

Joe came home from his visit with his parents. He said, "I felt God wanted our marriage saved, so I want to do what I can to save it. I promise not to be a workaholic any more." He was overwhelmed when Ellen told him about the inner vow she had renounced, and then she asked him to forgive her for her sins, which he did gladly.

You might want to examine yourself to see if you have made any inner vows after you were painfully hurt in your life. Check yourself for resentment, bitterness, and hate. These are sins that must be confessed to God and must be forgiven by Him. Jesus said, "Therefore I say to you, whatever things you ask when you pray, believe that you receive them, and you will have them. And whenever you stand praying, if you have anything against anyone, forgive him, that your Father in heaven may also forgive you your trespasses" (Mark 11:24–25).

In *Anatomy of an Illness* Norman Cousins described how he used ascorbic acid (vitamin C) in massive amounts and laughter to cure a life-threatening, painful stress disorder called collagen disease. Cousins wrote,

> The inevitable question arose in my mind. What about the positive emotions? If negative emotions produce negative changes in the body, wouldn't the positive emotions produce positive chemical changes? Is it possible that love, hope, faith, laughter, confidence, and the will to live have therapeutic value? Do chemical changes occur only on the downside?

Cousins systematically watched reruns of "Candid Camera," Charlie Chaplin movies, Marx Brothers' films, and other comedies to create laughter. He found that ten minutes of genuine belly laughter had an anesthetic effect and would give him at least two hours of pain-free sleep.

He stated,

> How scientific was it to believe that laughter, as well as the positive emotions in general, was affecting my body chemistry for the better? If laughter did in fact have a salutary effect on the body's chemistry, it seemed at least theoretically likely that it would enhance the system's ability to fight the inflammation. So we took sedimentation rate readings just before as well as several hours after the laughter episodes. The drop by itself was not substantial, but it held and was cumulative. I was greatly elated by the discovery that there is a physiologic basis for the ancient theory that laughter is good medicine.[13]

At a conference on the role of love and laughter in the healing process in 1982, Cousins told the audience that the body has its own internal apothecary, and without our knowledge, the body is writing prescriptions for itself all the time. Positive feelings such as joy and love have been shown to enhance the body's immune system.

I have used humor as a viable healing power in therapy and in lecturing. I love to laugh and to see people laugh. When I am to give an all-day seminar before a large audience, I know that if there is no humor, there will be lots of snoring. I realized this after years of preaching and seeing people doze off during the sermon. In fact, if all the people who slept in church were laid end to end, they would be more comfortable!

Humor is a marvelous way to attack the fear in phobic behavior. If a person can laugh at the fear, the fear dissolves. Try laughing out loud and then tell someone how fearful you are.

At a seminar in Maui we were discussing our fears when a dentist's wife said, "My greatest fear is of flying in an airplane."

I asked her, "How did you survive the long flight from Maui yesterday?"

"The old-fashioned way," she replied. "One old-fashioned after another. You will never know how hard it was to fly across the ocean and be terrified and feel that you must do something to help the pilot keep the plane in the air. I am already worrying about the flight home."

I agreed that she did need to help the pilot keep the plane in the air and asked her to visualize the following: There is a strong pole coming through the top of the roof to your seat. At the end of the pole are attached strong wires to the wings and to the nose and tail of the plane. Now you must hold the pole in your hands all the way home to help keep the plane in the air. If the stewardess asks you if you want something to drink or eat, you solemnly tell her "no thanks" because you can't take your hands off the pole as you and the pilot are keeping the plane in the air. She laughed at the idea and agreed to do it. She later wrote and told me what a safe flight she and her husband had, but it was hard work holding that pole all the time!

Fear is a reaction to things or experiences. Fear likes to control people, but fear can't stand to be laughed at and exposed to the light of day or to be faced head-on and challenged.

Since 1965, I have taught in dentistry, and I try to help dentists and their staffs deal effectively with hostile, fearful patients so no one will feel rejected. In one course, the dentists and their staffs were to practice learning how to take one second to think when given a hostile zinger and then respond with a "touch of class." The next month a young dentist reported that he had an interesting interaction with a hostile new patient. The patient had greeted the dentist with these words in a gruff, intimidating voice: "Doctor, I want you to know that I am the world's worst dental patient!" The dentist said, "Normally I would have been intimidated by that man, but I took a second to think before I responded and said, 'Well, at last we've met! I am the world's worst dentist!'"

There is healing power in humor. In the depression of the 1930s there wasn't much to laugh or smile about, yet that era produced some very fine comics. The times were so bad that only a good laugh could make a person feel better. The success of the television series "M.A.S.H." is due to the humor and laughter created by those who worked in that impossible, depressing wartime situation. Laughter is a sanity-saving release of tension. (In *The Art of Hanging Loose in an Uptight World,* I wrote more extensively on the use of humor in therapy.)

In the late eighteenth century in London, the entertainer Joseph Grimaldi made famous the clown character known as Joey. A physician who worked with many people suffering from depression, or melancholia as it was called then, would prescribe that these patients see performances of the Great Grimaldi. The depth of the melancholia determined how often they should go to the performances. The physician saw the patients improve as a result of their laughing.

As the story goes, one day a man appeared for an appointment with this physician; his melancholia was the worst case the doctor had ever seen. The doctor said, "Sir, you are in great luck because the Great Grimaldi is in town." He then began to prescribe how many times to see him when the patient interrupted, saying, "My dear doctor, I am the Great Grimaldi!"

We enter the world as helpless babies who must be touched and loved. This bonding in love is necessary to enable a baby to live and be healthy. If the infant does not receive this life-saving love, he may die.

The most powerful emotion for healing is love. The most beneficial emotion for a healthy life is love. The greatest gift from God is the gift of love. The gift of love from God is what the apostle Paul writes about in chapter 13 of 1 Corinthians. Man alone does not have the capability to love as described in Paul's hymn of love.

One of the greatest joys in life comes when I pray for a person who has been rejected, abused, and unloved. It is a joy to see the healing of deep woundedness. The power of the Holy Spirit brings the gift of God's love, which heals the wounded memories and emotions and fills the person with love.

NOTES

1. Thomas Verny with John Kolly, *The Secret Life of the Unborn Child* (New York: Summit Books, 1981).
2. Carlton Fredericks, *Psychonutrition* (New York: Grossett & Dunlap, 1970).
3. Ibid.

4. Jean Borysenko and David Myrin Borysenko, "On Psycho-neuroimmunology: How the Mind Influences Health and Disease, and How to Make the Influence Beneficial," *Executive Health* 19 (July 3, 1983).

5. James J. Lynch, *The Broken Heart* (New York: Basic Books, 1977).

6. Lawrence L. LeShan, *You Can Fight for Your Life* (New York: M. Evans & Co., 1977).

7. Ibid.

8. Irving Olye, *The New American Medicine Show* (Santa Clara, Calif.: Unity Press, 1979).

9. Sheldon B. Kopp, *If You Meet the Buddha on the Road, Kill Him!* (New York: Bantam, 1976).

10. C. S. Lewis, *A Grief Observed* (New York: Seabury Press, 1961).

11. John Powell, *Why Am I Afraid to Tell You Who I Am* (Allen, Tex.: Angus, 1969).

12. Loring Swaim, *Arthritis, Medicine, and the Spiritual Laws* (New York: Chilton, 1962).

13. Norman Cousins, *Anatomy of an Illness* (New York: Bantam, 1981).

CHAPTER SEVEN

THE HEALING MIND

There once was a very wise eighth-grade teacher who always seemed to have the right answer to any question asked by her students. Two of the boys wanted to devise a foolproof plan to show up the teacher in front of the class and prove that she wasn't all that wise. One day they caught a bird that was just learning to fly. The next day the boys approached the teacher, and one of them asked, "Miss Johnson, you are such a wise teacher; tell us if the bird in John's hand is dead or alive." If the teacher said the bird was alive, then John would squeeze the bird in his hand and show her a dead bird. If the teacher said the bird was dead, John would open his hand and let the bird fly away.

The teacher, who was very wise, replied, "Whether the bird is dead or alive, it is as John decides."

The more we explore the power of the decisions you and I make and how they affect our health and the more we learn about the healing power of the subconscious mind, the more we are aware of how little is known about the healing mind. Hans Selye always said that the key to preventing stress from becoming distress is the decision a person makes about what reaction he will choose.

A dentist friend told me of the time he suffered a coronary on his vacation to Europe. Back home his physician told him that one artery was closed to the heart, the second artery was almost completely closed, and the third artery was not far behind. He was told to go home and get his affairs in order because there was nothing to be done for him. In essence he was told to go home and expect to die soon.

After my friend had calmed down from receiving such depressing news, he made a decision to heal himself. He began to visualize the plaque in his arteries slowly crumbling away and more blood flowing through the arteries. He contacted Dr. Wilfred Shute in Canada about how many units of d-alpha-tocopherol of vitamin E he should take for his heart and plugged arteries. He took 800 units of vitamin E and 10,000 mg of vitamin C each day.

In seven weeks he went back to his surprised physician who told him that he thought he would have been dead by then. The physician was puzzled and amazed that not only was his patient alive, but he was improved. He asked the dentist what he was doing to cause the improvement, so my friend described his regimen. The physician scoffed at him and told him that that stuff wouldn't do any good. So my friend decided that he could do without that negative physician.

When I first met him at a dental meeting, he had just passed an extensive physical for a substantial life insurance policy with flying colors because his coronary disease was healed. If he had chosen to accept the deadly prognosis of his physician, he no doubt would have been very dead.

Franz Alexander, M.D., a pioneer in psychosomatic medicine writes, "The fact that the mind rules the body is, in spite of its neglect by biology and medicine, the most fundamental fact we know about the process of life."[1]

The hardest thing for a person to overcome in order to use

the healing power of the mind is a lifetime of negative thoughts, beliefs that have been programmed into the subconscious mind. As much as has been written about the power of positive thinking, I find that few people are positive thinkers; in fact, a person who lives with a positive mind-set is often viewed as though there is something wrong with him.

To tap into the healing power of the subconscious mind, we have to flush out our "stinking thinking" of negative thoughts and beliefs. We need to spot the negative tapes that are playing in the mind and disrupt them. In *The Art of Hanging Loose in an Uptight World* I wrote about negative tapes:

> A negative tape, as I use the concept, refers to a habitual thought pattern in which, once the "on button" is pushed, the negative thoughts soon evoke negative emotions, which recall a series of similar bad memories from the past that go on and on until they hypnotize you and claim power over your mind. If you've done any reading on the power of positive thinking, you know what a miraculous thing repetition can be. It convinces the subconscious, and the subconscious tells the conscious. Pretty soon your whole body is buying whatever the subconscious is selling.[2]

In attempting to change human behavior, we have made a common mistake in believing that if an individual only has enough information, he will change. If changing behavior were that simple, all a person would have to do to quit smoking would be to read the surgeon general's warning on a cigarette package that smoking cigarettes "may be hazardous to your health." If reasoning were the answer, everyone with this information would quit smoking.

The subconscious mind is very literal and if emotionally charged pictures or images are placed in the subconscious mind, change will take place. Also the more those images are repeated, the more energy is behind the suggestion and images.

Strong negative suggestions, commands, or injunctions will produce behavior in the opposite direction in the subconscious mind, which is a very important principle to remember. For instance, when you see a sign Wet Paint, what do you want to do? Touch it! The word *diet* is a very negative word in the subconscious mind. As soon as I go on a diet, I am intensely aware of all the commercials on TV for hamburgers, pizzas, fried chicken, and other fattening taste sensations.

I explained the power of the negative injunction on the subconscious mind at a retreat in North Carolina. A banker began to laugh and said, "That explains it. My wife and I were under a lot of stress, so we decided to take a weekend trip to a nice motel and relax. Before I left, I told our eighteen-year-old son, 'Don't take out the boat this weekend! I don't want to check into the motel, have the phone ring, and hear from the Coast Guard that you are missing in the inland waterways of North Carolina.' Well, just as I was carrying the suitcases into the motel, the clerk said, 'Are you Mr. Jackson?' I answered, 'Yes.' He said, 'You are wanted on the telephone.' I picked up the phone, and the Coast Guard informed me that our son and his friend were lost in our boat in the inland waterways! We rushed back home with a mixture of fear, anxiety, and anger. Why had he disobeyed me and the clear instructions I gave him? The Coast Guard had found our son and his friend before we got home. My son was sorry for what he had done. Afterward he said to me, 'Dad, I don't know why I took out the boat!' "

Negative, emotionally loaded words set off a negative reaction in the subconscious mind, in the emotions, and in the hormones within the body. Negative words can have the effect of a curse on a person's life. Words so emotionally loaded with fear and panic, such as *cancer* and *coronary,* cause the symptoms of the disease to accelerate. A person hears the word *cancer,* and the subconscious mind adds *death.*

It doesn't help when so many physicians have so few interpersonal skills in communicating to a patient the results of tests or surgery. Saying to a person, "Well, if I were you, I would go home and get my affairs in order" or "Your cancer is terminal," is an extremely frightening message and one that does nothing to inspire that patient to work in a positive way to fight that disease.

A woman called me in a state of panic after going to a physician concerning a lump in her breast. He crudely told her it was most likely malignant, even though he took no tissue for a biopsy, and began to describe in gory detail what a radical mastectomy was like. She pleaded with him to stop talking, but he was undaunted by her hysteria and continued to talk about survival rates and chemotherapy and its effects on the body. I tried to calm her down enough to understand that she should seek another medical opinion, which she did the next day. As it turned out, she did not need surgery because the tumor was not malignant.

A person in therapy told me of going for his annual physical. When the physician was going over the cardiogram, he muttered "oh, oh" to himself, but didn't explain what that was all about. The patient immediately imagined the worst but was fearful of facing the facts by asking the doctor what the "oh, oh" meant. In the weeks and months that passed, his anxiety over his heart increased, and he became very depressed, so much so that he had anxiety attacks. Finally, he went back to his doctor and said, "Tell me the truth about my heart. How serious a heart problem do I have?" The physician was perplexed and said, "You don't have a heart problem."

"But what was that 'oh, oh' all about when you were reading my cardiogram?" the man asked.

The doctor pulled out the cardiogram and went over it again, then realized he had muttered the "oh, oh" because the man's heart was in such good condition it was like that of a teenager!

Physicians are not gods; they have no special gift of discernment to know how long someone will live or how soon a person will die. No one should be told that death is inevitable. I have known some people with cancer who are filled with guilt if they live beyond the six months the physician told them they had to live.

In *The Healing Heart,* Norman Cousins tells of a physician's account of his rounds in a coronary care unit.

> I was examining a depressed appearing man. When I asked about the reason for the somber mood, he responded, "Doc, I don't think I am going to make it." To the question, "Why not?" he replied, "Well, the intern told that I have anterior wall infarct; the resident said I had a transmural heart attack; the cardiology fellow indicated that I experienced an occlusion of a major coronary artery, while the attending physician called it a coronary thrombosis and the nurse advised me not to ask questions. How can anyone survive so much heart damage?"[3]

In a moment with a few disastrous-sounding words, a physician can crush not only the will to live in a person, but also his belief in healing. That is the moment a person begins to die.

Physicians face a real problem as to how much and how to tell a person of all the risks and complications that can result from surgery. By law, the physicians have to do this to protect the patient and to prevent malpractice lawsuits. Sometimes surgeons and anesthesiologists become calloused by their work or do not realize the powerful emotional reaction that their words create in the subconscious mind prior to surgery. The panic and the depression created can push the person under anesthesia to a point beyond what the mind and body can tolerate, the heart stops, and the person dies.

During surgery, the subconscious mind is listening with its literalistic thought process, but the person will not be able to recall what was experienced in that state when consciousness is recovered. If, during surgery, the subconscious mind hears a joke and hears people laugh, the subconscious will interpret the joke and laughter as "I'm a joke and people are laughing at me." If there is anger and swear words are said during surgery, they will be received as pertaining to the person under anesthesia.

An oral surgeon and I were talking about this subject, and he recalled that during surgery on a person's mouth, a suspicious-looking cancerous tissue was discovered, a biopsy was taken, and surgery was stopped until a report was made. The technician returned from the laboratory and said, "It's malignant." The blood pressure of the person undergoing surgery immediately jumped 50 points!

Another oral surgeon told me about a little boy who was going into surgery to have his tonsils removed and to have corrective dental surgery. He kept saying, "Why do I have to die today?" No one paid any attention to the child's words. The operation was a success, but the boy died; he didn't come back from the anesthesia.

Recently there have been several articles written about the brain staying awake while people are anesthetized. Yet, operating room personnel often talk as if those having surgery are not listening. What is recorded in the unconscious mind can affect the outcome of surgery and recovery. The unconscious mind may understand and respond to meaning, form emotional responses, and guide most actions, largely independent of conscious awareness.

In one hospital's recovery room for gastrointestinal surgery, a strange form of diarrhea struck people when they became conscious. At a staff meeting to try to solve the mystery, one of the nurses recalled an anesthesiologist whispering in the ears of his patients, so it was agreed that they would have to talk with the physician and ask what he was telling them. He said he was concerned about postoperative gas and constipation for his patients, so he was whispering, "And when you wake up, you can have a bowel movement very easily with no gas or constipation." His patients obeyed his command, but the nurses said, "Please tell us in the future when you are going to do this so we can be better prepared!"

Dr. Bernie Siegel started a group called Exceptional Cancer Patients a few years ago after he discovered an innate healing potential that we all have—hope. His patients are given a bumper sticker with the motto "Anticipate Miracles." Siegel takes his love and optimism right into the operating room. He plays music during surgery and talks to his patients even when they are under anesthesia, telling them how well they are doing, how they will wake up comfortable, thirsty, and hungry.

He recalled,

> Once as I finished a difficult emergency abdominal operation on a young, very obese man, his heart stopped just as we were about to move him to the recovery room. He didn't respond to resuscitation. The anesthesiologist had given up and was walking out the door when I spoke out loud into the room, "Harry, it's not your time. Come on back." At once the cardiogram began to show electrical activity and the man ultimately recovered fully.[4]

Alyce Green says,

> The body does not seem to care about the scientific accuracy of the command or about the results per se; it simply carries out commands. Negative, destructive commands are followed, it seems, with as much success as positive commands. It is this

130

very fact that gives rise to the peculiar physiological behavior called psychosomatic diseases. Patients' visualization of success or failure, sickness or health, and ideas about their body and mind, together determine to an important extent what happens to them. The roots of psychosomatic disease lie in the unconscious and involuntary domain. It is the unconscious that gets the message from oneself and from other people and the environment.[5]

Let's examine how the subconscious mind works. It does not engage in analytical reasoning as the left hemisphere of the brain does. The decisions made are based on prior programming and the strength of the emotional image in the subconscious mind. The repeated suggestions and visualizations or mind pictures develop a pattern of behavior and change within a person. The subconscious mind is literal and reacts to the emotional input of thoughts and images it receives. The subconscious mind does not evaluate what it receives as to whether it is good or bad for the person. One of the most amazing powers of the subconscious mind is the ability to influence and change the autonomic nervous system and what that system controls.

Instructions to the subconscious mind can effect changes in the body via the autonomic nervous system, which creates change and control that the conscious mind cannot effect. Blood pressure can be lowered, tight bronchial tubes can open for deep breathing, bleeding and pain can be controlled in surgery, headaches relieved, muscles deeply relaxed so the tension stored in them is released, a reduction of stress hormones in the bloodstream can be achieved, anxiety lessened, and a deep peace of mind achieved. Many other things can occur through suggestions or visualizations to the unconscious mind. There is powerful energy in the healing mind!

I started a month-long promotional tour for a book in

Washington, D.C. I had Sunday to relax before I began a crazy schedule of radio and television shows, rushing to airports and other destinations on Monday. That Sunday I developed such a sore throat that I could not speak. Throughout the day, I took 10,000 mg of vitamin C and visualized my white cells attacking the germs causing my sore throat. By late afternoon, my throat was healed.

At home I ride an exercycle for an hour every day, which is boring to do except that I close my eyes, put some praise music on the stereo, and visualize myself traveling to the beautiful places Jeannie and I have visited. I also use this time to pray for people and for myself. It is a wonderful time to worship and praise God.

For ten years I played slow pitch softball with one of the church teams. I pitch because a "football" knee and other sports injuries do not allow me to do much running. One summer I decided to visualize hitting the ball. It worked! I was hitting over 700 most of the season. I had never hit a home run or visualized hitting one, so I said, "Why not?" I visualized the ball sailing over the fence time after time. Since I was playing on a team composed of college students, I believed it was up to the younger men to hit the home runs. After all, I was in my fifties! One night I said, "This is the night!" And sure enough, the ball went over the fence!

I told the team if I hit another home run during the rest of the season I would buy all the pizza that night. Well, the next game I hit one way over the center fielder's head. I wanted to stop at third base, but the third base coach said, "Keep on going, Doc." It was an expensive home run! The next game I was really loose and having fun. Two home runs in two games! So, I went to bat and cockily pointed my bat at the place I would hit a home run. The crowd loved it, and I hit it over the fence—just where I had pointed!

By then, I was visualizing in earnest on my exercycle, but

I was also thinking so hard and trying so hard that I never hit another homer that season. My batting average dropped under 700.

I was teaching a seminar on stress for physicians and dentists on a cruise several years ago. It wasn't until a year later that a dentist on the cruise told me that he had had a skin cancer on his face at the time of the cruise. He began to visualize the skin cancer being devoured by the T cells and macrophages, which looked like Pac-Men. What amazed him was that not only was the cancer healed, but during the healing process, it was reduced in size with "bites" in the half-moon shape made by Pac-Men!

Visualization and deep muscle relaxation are very well accepted now—that is, the process of seeing healing take place in the body. Dr. O. Carl Simonton, a radiation oncologist, developed a Cancer Counseling and Research Center in 1973 in Fort Worth, Texas (since 1981 it has been located in Dallas, Texas). He uses relaxation, mental imagery, and psychotherapy to help cancer patients learn to believe in their ability to recover from cancer. He directs patients to picture their cancer cells as vulnerable and disorganized and to visualize whatever treatment they are getting as strong and powerful, able to destroy the cancer without harming healthy cells. Patients are able to visualize the T cells, B cells, and macrophages devouring the cancer cells and flushing away dead and dying cancer cells. The cells of the immune system are emphasized, rather than chemotherapy or radiation, as the most powerful healing force. Each visualization session closes with the patient picturing himself strong, healthy, cancer-free, and achieving his life goals.[6]

I believe that people should be very careful about what they allow to enter the subconscious mind because the strength of the emotional images and the repeated programming of the subconscious mind determine how they will respond. For example, experts have estimated that by the time a young person has reached the age of eighteen, that person has witnessed eighteen thousand murders on television. If, as Marshall McLuhan believes, "the medium is the message," the message being programmed into young TV viewers is one of violence and murder. Is it any wonder that there has been a rapid increase in homicides by teenagers in the past twenty years?

Many young people listen to heavy metal rock by the hour. This type of music and videos, focusing on Satan, violence, hate, and death, is producing a shocking wave of murders and suicides, all involving satanic worship and occult practices.

In January 1988 the news media reported a story of a youth named Thomas Sullivan, age fourteen, who became obsessed with satanism. He stabbed his mother twelve times with his Boy Scout knife and then set fire to a sofa while his father and ten-year-old brother slept. The father, awakened by a smoke alarm, put out the fire with the help of a neighbor. The youth went into a neighbor's backyard and killed himself by slashing his wrists and cutting his throat.

Thomas Sullivan's Roman Catholic school had alerted his parents that he had passed a note detailing satanic rituals in reversed lettering. Some weeks before, his father said, the boy told a friend that Satan appeared to him in a vision, wearing his face and urging him to kill his family and preach satanism. He had become obsessed with satanic literature and heavy metal music.

There were no indications of problems with the boy until about a month before, when he began reading books on the occult and Satan worship. At that time, tension began to develop in the home.

Thomas Sullivan was described as a fine student and athlete at his high school. He was on the school wrestling team. A neighbor of the Sullivans said, "They were the kind of All-

American family everybody just dreams about." This story is not an isolated event.

Heavy metal rock, known for aggressive images and powerful rhythms, is a common thread in self-styled teen satanism. Drug use, occult books, satanic rituals, sacrifice of animals, and even human sacrifice play a part in it. The most destructive music is called black metal, which is blatantly satanic, with intensely violent lyrics that glorify torture, murder, and perversion. Some songs tell how to do specific satanic rituals.

This is a major problem. If you don't believe it, just look at the children's cartoons on Saturday morning and see how demonic they have become. Look at all the movies and televisions shows about supernatural evil, destruction, gruesome torture, and murder. These emotional images are programming subconscious minds for evil, and they will produce evil results. Programming of subconscious minds in this way is too serious a concern for me—or you—to ignore.

One of the most mysterious and yet powerful healing agents in the body is the placebo. The word *placebo* comes from the Latin verb, meaning "I shall please." The placebo is the ever-famous pill made from sugar that can do amazing healing feats as long as the person who receives it does not know it is a placebo. Belief in the placebo and belief in the physician produce a powerful healing relationship.

Studies have shown that a physician's belief and expectations of a drug's effectiveness can alter the outcome about 25 percent to 30 percent in either direction. Also, it has been reported that a drug works best when the physician's hopes for it are at their highest—when the drug is first released on the market and the studies in medical literature are primarily favorable, and before large numbers of side effects and ineffective applications have been reported. The Canadian physician,

Sir William Osler, remarked that new remedies should be used quickly "while they still are efficacious."[7]

A number of years ago, Dr. Philip West, a pioneer researcher of psychological factors in illness, was treating a man with severe cancer who begged to be given the experimental drug Krebiozen. At the time, Krebiozen was being hailed as a miracle cancer cure. After only one dose of the seemingly worthless drug, the patient's tumor masses "melted like snowballs on a hot stove." Whereas he had once needed an oxygen mask to breathe, he soon became so active that he again began piloting his own plane.

Shortly thereafter, the man read studies indicating that Krebiozen was ineffective. Immediately, his cancer began spreading again, and he was hospitalized. His physician, reacting to the dramatic turn of events, decided to test a hunch that he hoped would save his patient's life. He lied, telling the patient not to believe the studies, and promised treatment with a new, more potent Krebiozen. In fact, the man was given only water, but nevertheless his condition improved significantly. His recuperation continued until he read an article stating that the American Medical Association and the Food and Drug Administration had conclusively proved the worthlessness of Krebiozen. Several days later, the man died.[8]

I wonder if this man's belief in Krebiozen worked because it gave him a will to live, which then became a physical reality. We know now that the placebo triggers specific hormonal and biochemical changes in the body. Placebos have been shown to effect changes in electrocardiograms, the rate of stomach secretions, white blood cell counts, fever, blood cholesterol, dilation and constriction of pupils, and the stages of sleep.

Placebos are powerful even as painkillers. It is known that a placebo given as a painkiller will release an opiumlike substance called endorphin in the brain. As a painkiller, a placebo is about 56 percent as effective as morphine, codeine, or aspirin. It seems that the placebo effect may form the bedrock upon which the additional therapeutic effect of many pharmacologically active drugs is built.

How a placebo works is still largely a mystery, but its effectiveness is proof that there is no separation between mind and body. Norman Cousins notes, "The fact that a placebo will have no physiological effect if the patient knows it is a placebo only confirms something about the capacity of the human body to transform hope into tangible and essential biochemical change. The placebo is the doctor who resides within."[9]

Dr. Jerome D. Frank of Johns Hopkins University School of Medicine told students at graduation exercises in 1975 that any treatment of an illness that does not also minister to the human spirit is grossly deficient. Dr. Frank referred to a study of 176 cases of cancer that remitted without surgery, radiation, or chemotherapy. The question raised by these episodes was whether a powerful factor in those remissions may have been the patients' deep belief that they were going to recover and their equally deep convictions that their doctors also believed they were going to survive.[10]

Bernie Siegel writes,

Physicians tend to be more logical, statistical, and rigid, and less inclined to have hope than their patients. When the physician runs out of remedies, they're likely to give up. They must realize, however, that lack of faith in the patient's ability to heal can severely limit that ability. We should never say, "There's nothing more I can do for you." There's always something more we can do, even if it's only to sit down, talk, and help the patient hope and pray."[11]

One of the great mysteries in medicine is how to explain a spontaneous remission of a disease that should have killed a person. Why do two people with the same kind of cancer have such different outcomes? The one survives because of a powerful will to live and a belief in healing while the other person dies because of surrender to hopelessness, helplessness, and death in a self-fulfilling prophecy. I am sure that if a study was done on the immune cells and healing hormones in both people, there would be a significantly lower count in the person who surrenders to hopelessness and helplessness.

Elmer and Alyce Green of the Menninger Institute studied cases of spontaneous remission from cancer. They discovered that patients had used everything from a pilgrimage to Lourdes to an Arizona grapefruit juice cure. Where they went for healing or what they took for healing was not the reason for the spontaneous remission, however. (By the way, the term *spontaneous remission* is the medical term for "we are ignorant of the cause of recovery.") The Greens searched for a common factor in the spontaneous remission of cancer, and they found that to be a dramatic change in the attitude of the patient to one of hope and positive feelings. [12]

Carl Simonton's work with cancer patients reveals that the most significant finding in 152 cases was that a positive attitude toward treatment was a better predictor of response to treatment than was the severity of the disease. Negative beliefs can be powerful in starting any self-fulfilling prophecies of death. [13]

Arnold Hutschnecker writes, "Anxiety is one of the signs that the will to live is under attack. Depression goes a step further; it indicates a partial surrender to death." [14]

Consider this biblical story:

Now there is in Jerusalem by the Sheep Gate a pool, which is called in Hebrew, Bethesda, having five porches. In these lay a great multitude of sick people, blind, lame, paralyzed, waiting for the moving of the water. For an angel went down at a certain time into the pool and stirred up the water; then whoever stepped in first, after the stirring of the water, was made well of whatever disease he had. Now a certain man was there who had an infirmity thirty-eight years. When Jesus saw him lying there, and knew that he already had been in that condition a long time, He said to him, "Do you want to be made well?"

The sick man answered Him, "Sir I have no man to put me into the pool when the water is stirred up; but while I am coming, another steps down before me."

Jesus said to him, "Rise, take up your bed and walk." And immediately the man was made well, took up his bed, and walked (John 5:2-9).

The man by the pool never said, "Yes, I want to be healed," but instead told Jesus how he could never get into the pool in time when the water was stirred up. Only when he obeyed the command of Jesus to stand up was he healed.

One of the most important questions I ask a person who comes for therapy is, "Do you want to be healed?" I never assume that because someone comes for help, the desire to be healed is present. People do choose not to be well, not to be healed, and not to live. People have the right to be sick and remain sick. In the movie *Resurrection,* a young woman on a stretcher was brought to a woman with the gift of healing. The healer looked at her for a while, refused to try to heal her, and sent her home. When asked why she didn't heal the woman, the healer replied, "Some people need their illness since it is the only way they can get love."

A man confined to a wheelchair because of having multiple sclerosis told me of the countless healing services he had attended, but he had never felt any power of the Holy Spirit. He was a Christian minister. I asked him, "Do you want to be healed?" At first he was stunned by the question, so I let him think about it for a week. The following week he confessed, "I don't want to be healed. If I were healed, I would have to give up my disability income, and then I would have to find a church to serve and get back in all the stress that caused my MS. My wife and I live quite comfortably now because we have so little stress."

Do you want to be healed? This is the most important question to ask someone who is sick. It confronts a sick person with a choice and the responsibility of playing a major role in the healing. It sounds like such an easy, obvious question to answer, "Of course I want to be healed!" A primary reason this question is so difficult to answer is that we have been programmed to view ourselves as helpless victims with little, if any, responsibility for getting well. It is almost automatic to give all responsibility for healing to the physician. It's like saying, "Well, I'm sick; you're the doctor, so now heal me."

Unfortunately, the training of a physician leads to the attitude of putting the physician on a pedestal; in effect, the healing of the patient is the *doctor's* responsibility. The patient is to do what the doctor tells him without asking too many questions. It is the relationship of the "healer" to the "sickee"; the "healer" has all the responsibility, and the "sickee" has none.

The word *patient* conveys negative images because it describes a relationship in which the person with the illness is a passive subject who waits for the doctor to perform a healing. If a patient dies, the doctor reacts as if he or she has failed. A doctor's greatest fear is the death of a patient. I have talked with numerous doctors about how they feel when a patient dies. Each one viewed the event as a personal failure. I believe if a doctor has done all that can be done to save a person's life, and that person dies, the doctor hasn't failed. The doctor should remember that even God allows people to die, so maybe he or she should quit upstaging God.

As a psychotherapist, I work only with people who will accept responsibility for their lives, their problems, and their healing. I work as a facilitator of change, but I will never accept responsibility for the person's change. I don't even go by the title "doctor" in order to keep out of the one-up position as the "healer" and put the person in the one-down position as a "sickee."

Norman Cousins has become a modern hero in medicine, not because he is a great physician, but because he is a journalist who cured himself of collagen disease. The conclusions he draws from his healing experience are these:

One, the will to live is not a theoretical abstraction, but a physiologic reality with therapeutic characteristics. The second is that I was incredibly fortunate to have as my doctor a man who knew that his biggest job was to encourage to the fullest the patient's will to live and to mobilize all the natural resources of body and mind to combat disease—and, though, I can't be sure of this point, I have a hunch he believed that my own total involvement was a major factor in my recovery.

People have asked what I thought when I was told by the specialists that my disease was progressive and incurable. The answer is simple. Since I didn't accept the verdict, I wasn't trapped in the cycle of fear, depression, and panic that frequently accompanies a supposedly incurable illness.[15]

Dr. Thomas Haskett, chief of psychiatry at Massachusetts General Hospital, has long had a special interest in the personality characteristics that help individuals survive extreme adversity. One of his favorite studies has been of the fighter pilots of World War I. Aviation was in its infancy. Many of the aspiring pilots barely made it off the ground, and one in four was killed during training in the unreliable planes. Many more lost their lives in combat.

Those who survived World War I went on to triumph over other adversities, such as the stock market crash in 1929, the depression, and World War II, in which many enlisted. They survived the death of a loved one or divorce.

Haskett interviewed forty of these pilots when they were in

their late seventies and early eighties. Many of the traits he observed repeatedly were optimism, a sense of humor, and the ability to reduce or abolish worry or fear, even in times of great stress. Haskett called them the deniers—people who minimize the seriousness of their condition through hope, optimism, and humor. Denial has been a defense mechanism noted by other investigators of individuals coping with personal difficulties including serious illnesses such as cancer and heart attacks.[16]

Bernie Siegel has discovered three types of cancer patients:

> About 15% to 20% of all patients unconsciously, or even consciously, wish to die. On some level they welcome cancer or another serious illness as a way to escape their problems through death or disease. These are the patients who show no signs of stress when they find out their diagnosis. If you ask them how they are, they say, "Fine." And what is troubling them? "Nothing."
>
> In the middle of the spectrum of patients is the majority, about 60% to 70%. They are like actors auditioning for a part. They perform to satisfy the physician. These are the people who, given a choice, would rather be operated on than actively work to get well.
>
> At the other extreme are the 15% to 20% who are exceptional. They are not auditioning; they're being themselves. Exceptional patients refuse to be victims. They educate themselves and become specialists in their own care. They question the doctor because they want to understand their treatment and participate in it. They demand dignity, personhood, and control, no matter what the course of the disease.[17]

After I ask if someone wants to be healed, I ask, "Do you believe you can be healed?" A person may want to be healed, but is having a hard time believing he can be healed. This believing in healing is learning the "faith walk." What is faith?

"Faith is the substance of things hoped for, the evidence of things not seen" (Heb. 11:1).

Luke tells about incredible faith in the account of the healing of ten lepers:

> Now it happened as He went to Jerusalem that He passed through the midst of Samaria and Galilee. Then as He entered a certain village, there met Him ten men who were lepers, who stood afar off. And they . . . said, "Jesus, Master, have mercy on us!"
>
> So . . . He said to them, "Go, show yourselves to the priests." And so it was that as they went, they were cleansed.
>
> And one of them, when he saw that he was healed, returned, and with a loud voice glorified God, and fell down on his face at His feet, giving Him thanks. And he was a Samaritan.
>
> So Jesus answered and said, "Were there not ten cleansed? But where are the nine? Were there not any found who returned to give glory to God except this foreigner?" (Luke 17:11–18).

I am going to give you a different understanding of the healing of the ten lepers than you have ever heard before. Lepers were banished to live out in the desert, away from family and friends; they led desolate lives of dying a little bit each day as the leprosy ravaged their bodies. There was no cure for leprosy, no hope, only death. When the ten lepers saw Jesus at a distance, they cried out for mercy. They knew Jesus could heal the sick, even those with leprosy.

Jesus looked at them. Can't you imagine what love and compassion was in His look and how His loving heart must have gone out to them? Yet Jesus did not heal them on the spot. The disciples, remember, had asked how they could receive more faith, and Jesus was going to show them a powerful example of faith.

At that time the priests were the public health officers, and they were the only ones who could issue a healed leper a statement he could show people as evidence he was healed. This point is usually missed. The ten lepers wanted to be healed and believed they would be healed because they started toward Jerusalem to see the priests while they still had leprosy. They obeyed the command of Jesus that they would be healed. They did not react the way most of us would by saying, "I'm not going to Jerusalem until I'm healed; I'm going to wait to be healed."

And as they were going to Jerusalem, their leprosy disappeared. What joy and thanksgiving and praise must have come from their hearts and their lips! Why did the Samaritan return to Jesus and give thanks? For a very obvious reason. As a despised Samaritan, he couldn't see the priests in Jerusalem, for he was not a Jew. So he returned to Samaria. Remember, this encounter with Jesus and the ten lepers took place on the border between Samaria and Galilee. As he was heading home, the Samaritan ran into Jesus and His disciples and fell down in the dust before Jesus, thanking Him for what He had done.

We are such an instant "now" society that it is very difficult to walk out a healing over a period of time. For the whole person to be healed, it often takes a lot of hard work to get all the junk out of our lives, our emotions, our relationships, our minds, our spiritual lives, before we can be healed physically and keep our healing by making the changes in our life-style that will prevent us from being sick again.

Do you believe that you can be healed if you walk out your hope? "Now faith is the substance of things hoped for, the evidence of things not seen" (Heb. 11:1).

I wrote these words in *Can You Wait Till Friday?*:

The psychology of hope is believing in people and realizing that people have within themselves the power to change. Hope is trusting people to grow in beauty, creativity, sensitivity and aliveness. The basis of a person's life is hope. Where there is hope, there is life, and not the other way around. When there is no hope for the future, there is no power for the present. Once the candle of hope is extinguished, the road is all downhill.[18]

A psychology of hope is powerful when a person can finally say, "Here I am, God help me!" There is a sense of deep relief to let go of our need to control God, to release our fears, resentments, doubts, and any other barrier within us so that the Holy Spirit may flow within us and bring such gifts of the Spirit as hope, joy, peace, healing, and love. This letting go and letting God is not to be confused with being resigned to depression and death and giving up the will to live and the belief in healing. Healing is a cooperative venture in which the person still fights for life—obeys the command of Jesus to take action where there is yet sickness. When Jesus told the man crippled for thirty-eight years to get up, roll up his mat, and go home, the man obeyed Jesus' command. He was still crippled, but as he obeyed, he was healed. The ten lepers were healed as they walked out their healing while they still had leprosy.

Norman Cousins observes,

We must learn to never underestimate the capacity of the human mind and body to regenerate—even when the prospects seem most wretched. The most important thing I have learned about the power of belief is that an individual patient's attitude toward serious illness can be as important as medical help. It would be a serious mistake to bypass or minimize the need for scientific treatment, but that treatment will be far more effective if people put their creative hopes, their faith, and their confidence fully to work in behalf of their recovery.[19]

NOTES

1. Franz Alexander, *Psychosomatic Medicine* (New York: Norton, 1950).
2. Ken Olson, *The Art of Hanging Loose in an Uptight World* (New York: Fawcett, 1974).
3. Norman Cousins, *The Healing Heart* (New York: Norton, 1983).
4. Bernie S. Siegel, *Love, Medicine, and Miracles* (New York: Harper & Row, 1986).
5. Elmer Green and Alyce Green, *Beyond Biofeedback* (New York: Delta, 1977).
6. O. Carl Simonton, Stephanie Matthews-Simonton, and James L. Creighton, *Getting Well Again* (New York: Bantam, 1978).
7. "Placebo," *Executive Health Report* 23 (October 1981).
8. Bruno Klopfer, "Psychological Variables in Human Cancer," *Journal of Projective Techniques* 21 (1957): 337–39.
9. Norman Cousins, *Anatomy of an Illness* (New York: Bantam, 1981).
10. Jerome Frank, "The Faith That Heals," *Johns Hopkins Medical Journal* 137 (1975): 127–31.
11. Siegel, Ibid.
12. Green and Green, Ibid.
13. Simonton, Ibid.
14. Arnold S. Hutschnecker, *The Will to Live* (New York: Cornerstone Library, 1974).
15. Cousins, *Anatomy of an Illness,* Ibid.
16. "Hope: That Sustainer of Man," *Executive Health* 20 (December 1983).
17. Siegel, Ibid.
18. Ken Olson, *Can You Wait Till Friday?* (Phoenix: O'Sullivan-Woodside, 1975).
19. Norman Cousins, *Human Options* (New York: Norton, 1981).

CHAPTER EIGHT

SPIRITUALLY ALIVE
AND HEALTHY

Religious activity is my favorite escape from God.
—*ANTHONY de MELLO*

"Each bird whistles through his own beak" is one of my favorite sayings. It has never been more true than in what I reveal of my own spirituality in this chapter. I fully expect that some of you will disagree with what I say, others will not know what to think, and some will hear me and rejoice.

I am a Christian who works as a psychologist and a pastor for the Center for Living with a special ministry of healing the whole person—emotional, mental, spiritual, and physical—according to the teachings of Jesus Christ. I am a Christian pilgrim who is in the never-ending process of spiritual growth. I know that I have a long way to go and God is not finished with me yet, so bear that in mind.

The spiritual dimension of the human being is the most neglected area in health and healing. I believe that spiritual health is the foundation on which a life of positive wellness is built. There is a direct relationship between spiritual health and emotional, mental, and physical well-being. Later on in this chapter I will show you why this is true.

Psychology means the "study of the soul" in Greek, and *psychotherapy* means the "therapy of the soul." But woe be to the psychologist who, in the course of therapy, uses spiritual means for the healing of spiritual problems. If the State Board of Psychologist Examiners hear about a psychologist using spiritual means, such as the Holy Spirit, in therapy, they could try to take away his license since psychologists are not trained to believe in the spiritual nature of man, much less use spiritual means for healing spiritual ills.

In 1956 when I first read Viktor Frankl's book *The Doctor and the Soul,* it was a welcome breath of fresh air and hope. In the introduction Frankl wrote, "Man lives in three dimensions: the somatic, the mental, and the spiritual. The spiritual dimension cannot be ignored for it is what makes us human. To be concerned about the meaning of life is not necessarily a sign of disease or of neurosis."

" 'It is true,' Freud once declared in conversation, 'humanity has always known that it possesses a spirit; it was my task to show that it has instincts as well.' But I feel that humanity has demonstrated ad nauseam in recent years that it has instincts and drives. Today it appears more important to remind man that he has a spirit, that he is a spiritual being."[1]

In Genesis we read,

> Then God said, "Let Us make man in Our image, according to Our likeness; let them have dominion over the fish of the sea, over the birds of the air, and over the cattle, over all the earth and over every creeping thing that creeps on the earth." So God created man in His own image; in the image of God He created him; male and female He created them (1:26–27).

God is a spiritual being, and man is a spiritual being, created in the image and likeness of God. God created man out of love and for a relationship between God and man so man could communicate, worship, and praise God.

In the Western world we have developed a belief system

that determines what is to be included and what is to be excluded. The secular materialism of this belief system states that we live in a world in which truth is arrived at through scientific means, measurement, and rational thought. It is a closed universe in which the supernatural is excluded, so the supernatural is naturally unnatural.

The Western worldview has been strongly influenced by the philosopher René Descartes and the physics of Isaac Newton:

> To Descartes the material world was a machine and nothing but a machine. There was no purpose, life, or spirituality in matter. Nature worked according to mechanical laws, and everything in the material world could be explained in terms of the arrangement and movement of its parts. This mechanical picture of nature became the dominant paradigm of science in the period following Descartes. It guided all scientific observation and the formulation of all theories of natural phenomena.[2]

The Western world became overly enamored with the scientific method of mathematical, analytical reason and reduction of parts to smaller and smaller subparts. For many people, this belief system became the only way of truth and knowledge.

What about knowledge gained by direct experience, such as emotions, spirit, God, visions, dreams, intuition, and the evidence of the five senses? According to the scientific, mechanistic worldview of Descartes and Newton, experiential knowledge must be disregarded if the worldview depicted is irrational or illogical.

"I don't think anything has changed our world more during the past four hundred years than the obsession of scientists with measurement and quantification," says British psychiatrist R. D. Laing.[3]

The Christian theology of the Western world has been seduced into a worldview of a closed universe in which the supernatural powers of God and Satan are locked out. The church has its intellectualized, rational theology, doctrines, and creeds, which teach Christians how to live and what to believe about God. The result is the denial of the activity of the supernatural in our world. Thomas Aquinas based his theology on the philosophy of Aristotle, who believed in a closed universe in which there was no room for a separate realm of the spiritual, nor was there need of the spiritual realm because man can use his reason to understand and control his world.

Philip Melanchthon, a theologian who was a close friend of Martin Luther, also based his theology on the philosophy of Aristotle. Is it any wonder that Western Christian theology is long on head knowledge but void of spirituality and the supernatural, such as God, angels, Satan, and demons? Is it any wonder that belief in divine healing is viewed as absurd before it can be investigated?

James J. Lynch writes,

> With the growth of scientific medicine in the twentieth century, two things occurred. First of all, people saw less need for this type of "magical" religious healing. Secondly, and perhaps of greater significance, churches themselves adopted objectivity as a means par-excellence for examining their own beliefs. This latter stance of objectivity, assessing faith systems and theology, I believe, proved to be an especially disruptive posture for religion, and one that had immediate consequences. These two changes brought about a dramatic decline in the healing aspects of religion, as well as a consequent decline in the interest in religion itself.[4]

When I went to seminary, I was taught that the days of miracles of healing were over because after the apostolic age God recalled the Holy Spirit who was responsible for those signs and wonders. Once the church was established, the signs and wonders were no longer needed. The people had the Holy Bible, and the Holy Spirit was recalled. It was felt that the Holy Spirit was no longer needed in the church. This theological viewpoint is called the theory of dispensationalism. It is still being taught in seminaries and preached from pulpits in most of our mainline Christian churches. In the closed universe belief system it can be concluded that God doesn't work here any more.

Morton Kelsey's review of the most comprehensive survey of contemporary theology by John Macquarrie's *Twentieth Century Religious Thought* reveals that Christian healing is simply overlooked today. Of the 150 theologians reviewed in his book, not one emphasizes the effect of man's religious life on his mental and physical well-being. Few religious writers even bother with arguments against healing.[5]

There is no divine healing without the power and presence of the Holy Spirit. The Holy Spirit is the spiritual presence of God in this world, but if your belief system in a closed universe does not allow the presence and experience of the power of the Holy Spirit, you do not believe in divine healing, much less can you pray expectantly for God to heal a sick person. In fact, praying to God in a closed universe is rather a fruitless activity. Even if your prayer is heard by God, you cannot expect Him to answer your prayer or intervene in your life.

Belief systems determine what you receive into your world of reality. If you hear or read something that doesn't fit your belief system, it simply is not received and believed.

I firmly believe that there is little teaching and preaching about the power and presence of the Holy Spirit in churches because it doesn't fit our belief systems. I honestly believe churches that open their worship services, "In the name of the Father, and the Son, and the Holy Spirit," would be more accurate if they opened their service, "In the name of the Father, and the Son, and What's His Name." Some ministers and church members are more afraid of the Holy Spirit than they are of Satan, who most don't believe really exists anyway.

A. W. Tozer has written,

Satan has opposed the doctrine of the Spirit-filled life about as bitterly as any doctrine there is. He has confused it, opposed it, surrounded it with false notions and fears. He has blocked every effort of the church of Christ to receive from the Father his divine and blood-bought patrimony. The church has tragically neglected this great liberating truth—that there is now for the child of God a full, wonderfully and completely satisfying anointing with the Holy Spirit. The Spirit-filled life is not a special, deluxe edition of Christianity. It is part and parcel of the total plan of God for His people.[6]

Now, how do you react to these words about the Holy Spirit and the Spirit-filled life? Do you receive them, or do you feel uncomfortable hearing about the Holy Spirit and being empowered and filled with the Holy Spirit? It all depends on your belief system. I hope and pray that you will be open to growth in your spiritual life and to being led and filled by the Holy Spirit. I don't know how to be spiritual unless the Holy Spirit comes to me, fills me, and unites with my spirit.

A large majority of Christians in the Western world believe in the supernatural only in the transcendent world beyond our world, like heaven, but exclude the supernatural on earth. For peoples of the Third World countries of Africa, Asia, Central and South America, the supernatural is included as natural in their life on earth. Thus, the supernatural is naturally natural.

Many of the missionaries who are sent to Third World countries are confronted with people who believe in spirits, good and evil, in their daily lives, and want help in casting out the evil spirits in their village. They want the missionary to pray for the sick people in their village. Now, if you were that missionary, how would you feel about expelling the village of evil spirits and praying for a sick person? If your theology doesn't include expelling demons, breaking the curses of a medicine man, and praying for the sick, how effective would you be as a missionary to these people for whom the spirit world is very much a part of their daily experience?

Not only do different worldviews affect the spiritual, but there is also a real difference between being religious and being spiritual. Religion has to do with man's attempt to go to God and establish a relationship with God and be saved. This saving relationship is achieved through developing religious ceremonies, rituals, rules of do's and don'ts, and specific doctrines and creeds. The focus of religious activities is to lead a person to live a holy life and become acceptable to God as a result of the religious activities and beliefs.

The only problem is that no one is perfect because "man is born to goof." I should keep the Ten Commandments; I should love my God with all my heart, soul, and mind; and I should love my neighbor as myself. The "shoulds" of love sound wonderful, but there is no power in me to transform myself into this loving person. It is very hard to love even the members of a family, much less an enemy or two!

Religious legalism causes people either to quit trying to be religious and feel overwhelmed with guilt and fear or to become very pious and filled with self-righteous pride.

Remember, the very religious scribes, Pharisees, and priests, the religious "fat cats," were the ones who had Jesus crucified. It is no wonder that Jesus' harshest words were to these religious leaders: "Woe to you, scribes and Pharisees, hypocrites! For you are like whitewashed tombs which indeed appear beautiful outwardly, but inside are full of dead men's bones and all uncleanness. Even so you also outwardly appear righteous to men, but inside you are full of hypocrisy and lawlessness" (Matt. 23:27–28).

To me, the good news of Christianity is that of God's love coming to me, though I can never be good enough or religious enough to earn my salvation and establish a good relationship with God by my own efforts. Christianity is God-centered activity. It means God coming to me with unconditional love in Jesus Christ because I am a broken, wounded, unworthy sinner needing healing and redemption. In short, the basis of my relationship with God is not my religious righteousness but my own messed-up and wounded self.

I am so thankful that in my formative years I belonged to Grace Lutheran Church in Phoenix where Pastor "Pete" preached and taught the grace of God, God's love in action, and justification by faith in Jesus Christ alone as the way of salvation. I never was taught about a God of fear and guilt; I knew only about His grace and forgiveness.

For me, the spiritual work is one in which I experience the presence of the Holy Spirit in worship, in prayer, in reading the Word of God, in witnessing to others about the great love of God revealed in my personal Savior Jesus Christ. I do not believe in a closed universe in which the supernatural is not present, but my worldview is one in which the supernatural is naturally natural. When I pray for the sick, I first pray for the Holy Spirit, and I experience the anointing of the Holy Spirit—and so does the person I am praying with. Through the presence and power of the Holy Spirit, I see the "brokenhearted healed and the captives set free." God has not run out of power. Jeremiah heard the Lord say to him, "Behold, I am the LORD, the God of all flesh. Is there anything too hard for Me?" (Jer. 32:27).

My accepting Jesus as my Savior is first made possible by the leading of the Holy Spirit who enables me to accept Jesus as

Lord. It is through the ongoing work of the Holy Spirit that I become a new person in Christ: "But the fruit of the Spirit is love, joy, peace, longsuffering, kindness, goodness, faithfulness, gentleness, self-control" (Gal. 5:22–23).

A sad commentary on most Christian churches and Christians themselves is the pervasiveness of spiritual deadness. George Gallup, in his report "1984 Religion in America," said, "Religion is growing in importance among Americans but morality is losing ground. . . . There is very little difference in the behavior of the churched and unchurched on a wide range of items including lying, cheating, and pilferage."

The spiritual climate in the United States is one of an ever-increasing darkness, destruction, and moral decay. Self-centered "me-ism," sin-drome, and pleasure seeking are evident. There is such a deep spiritual vacuum in so many lives that people turn to drugs to fill the emptiness and provide a temporary, chemical sense of well-being. It is mind-boggling to realize that more money is made on illicit drugs than is produced by General Motors and by agriculture in this country. I firmly believe the drug problem is with users, and it is basically a spiritual problem.

These words are very accurate in describing our times:

> Do not love the world or the things in the world. If anyone loves the world, the love of the Father is not in him. For all that is in the world—the lust of the flesh, the lust of the eyes, and the pride of life—is not of the Father but is of the world (1 John 2:15–16).

If you think things haven't drastically changed for the worse, just look at the changes in major problems in public schools from 1940 to 1988.[7]

Top Problems in 1940	Top Problems Today— 1988
1. Talking	1. Drug Abuse
2. Chewing Gum	2. Alcohol Abuse
3. Making Noise	3. Pregnancy
4. Running in the Halls	4. Suicide
5. Getting Out of Line	5. Rape
6. Wearing Improper Clothing	6. Robbery
7. Not Putting Paper in Wastebasket	7. Assault

A few years ago Karl Menninger wrote a book called *Whatever Happened to Sin?* Well, it didn't go away. It's still here. Sin is the result of a broken relationship with God and our fellow man. It comes out of rebellion and pride.

Another sign of the increasing darkness over our land is the rise of satanism, witchcraft, and other occult practices. What do we do about this supernatural evil that is making itself more visible? Rational explanations can't account for the bizarre, horrifying evidence of satanic, ritualistic, sexual abuse of children, people, and animals sacrificed at a Black Mass to worship Satan.

Psychiatrist Scott Peck wrote a chilling book, *People of the Lie,* in which he calls for the development of a psychology of evil that must also be a healing psychology:

> Finally, of course, a psychology of evil must be a religious psychology. By this I do not mean it must embrace a specific theology. I do mean, however, that it must not only embrace valid insights from all religious traditions but must also recognize the reality of the "Supernatural." And, as I have said, it must be a science in submission to love and the sacredness of life. It cannot be a purely secular psychology.[8]

156

The secular news media are reporting more frequently on satanic activities. On May 17, 1988, *The Arizona Republic* reported on the desecration of three crypts in a Phoenix cemetery in which two bodies were decapitated and a third body was cremated by alleged satanists.

Geraldo Rivera recently had a television show about parents whose children had been sexually abused by satanists in preschool nurseries. "In San Francisco, an eight year old girl describes to police a candlelit room where a crucifix hangs upside down. A baby's legs are burned in fire and the crying infant is laid on a blanket. With the father guiding her, the girl stabs the child through the navel and drinks the blood."[9]

The news media and police departments are very concerned about satanism, ritualistic sexual abuse, and ritualistic killings. Ironically, on the whole, Christian pastors and churches are silent about satanism and witchcraft. When I was in Tucson visiting my son, Danny, and his wife and children in February 1988, there was a full page on the rise of satanism, satanic murders, heavy and black metal music, and so on. That evening when I got home, I saw that the "Religion" section of *The Arizona Republic* had a featured article, "The Devil Is Losing His Sizzle." The secular press deals with the satanic, but the sacred press denies the reality of Satan and satanism.

I have worked with people in therapy who have been ritualistically sexually abused, tortured, left for dead, and offered to Satan at a Black Mass. The horrible memories that are released over time are unbelievable. I pray for the inner healing of these nightmarish memories and pain. There are also demonic spirits that must be expelled before these tragically wounded people can be healed and made whole.

Now, what does all this about Satan and demons have to do with spiritual health and wellness? I believe in preventive medicine, and this concerns preventive spiritual medicine. People in our country are spiritually hungry and seeking spiritual experiences of the supernatural. The seekers have often been active members in Christian churches, but they have grown restless because they have not been receiving spiritual food, so they often turn to other sources to satisfy their spiritual hunger.

There is a sensational rise of interest in the occult, which is called the New Age movement, with actress Shirley MacLaine as one of its most visible spokespersons. This "new spirituality" is really not all that new because it includes belief in seances, astral travel, Hindu reincarnation, Hindu karma, channeling energy from the "God Force," and the concept that everyone is God. This type of belief began as far back as the temptation in the Garden of Eden when the serpent said to Eve that she wouldn't die if she ate the fruit: "For God knows that in the day you eat of it your eyes will be opened, and you will be like God, knowing good and evil" (Gen. 3:5).

An article in *U.S. News & World Report* stated,

From Manhattan to Malibu, a big and bizarre business is springing up as Americans look for supernatural answers to real life problems. Psychics are collecting up to $250.00 an hour for making predictions, and channeling advice from entities, alleged spirits from another world or another time. The number of channels in California is above 1,000. One of them, Jack Pursel of San Francisco, grosses more than $1,000,000 a year in seminars, counseling, and video cassettes as the medium for a spirit known as Lazaris, "consummate friend."[10]

Even the respected *Wall Street Journal* on April 1, 1981, had a feature article entitled "For Personal Insights, Some Try Channels. Out of This World Communicating With Spirits is Becoming a New Rage for New Age Philosophers."

In the August 2, 1986, edition of *The Arizona Republic* was a story of a female Episcopal priest who resigned from the church she was serving in Issaquah, Washington, because she refused to renounce the teaching of the spirit named Jonah that spoke through her. Jonah, who claims to have lived in Jesus' time, said that Jesus married a Druid princess, was a father, and did not die on the cross but had a three-day out-of-body experience.

The New Age occult explosion is based on the desire for new spiritual experiences and power and on pride. For most, there is no thought of the danger of using crystals for healing; relying on pyramid power; going to seances; seeking spiritual "guides" for one's life; playing with a Ouija board; channeling energy from an unknown source, psychics, astrology, psychic healers, TM, or astral travel (leaving the physical body); playing a game of Dungeons and Dragons (a course in witchcraft); and progressing to witchcraft or Satan worship.

What is the danger? Any time you seek power from the kingdom of darkness, you open yourself up to be filled with evil spirits, which may for a time say they are your spirit guides, or from the spirit of a person you contacted through hypnotic regression to past lives. You may not believe this could happen to you, that you could be filled with demons this way, but I have experienced the power and presence of demonic spirits through the process of casting out demons in the name and authority of Jesus Christ.

I have been trained in clinical hypnosis, but I will no longer use hypnosis as a form of therapy because it opens up the subconscious mind not only to my suggestions but to suggestions of other people whose intentions are to destroy. Therefore, I am also very much against subliminal tapes in advertising. The area of mind control is very dangerous. The Russians are far ahead of us in working out techniques for mind control.

One of my most difficult cases of delivering a person intent on evil purposes began with a woman who had gone for hypnosis for over a year in which, under hypnotic trance, she was opened to demonic possession and led to acts that violated her own beliefs.

The argument rages as to whether or not a person will do something against his will while in a state of hypnosis. The answer is yes. Using drugs, you can produce under hypnosis a state of mind control, which will cause a person to carry out assignments without his conscious will being involved.

I have deprogrammed someone who was under mind control and had been assigned to carry out an evil action. This was *not* a violent person but one who had been seduced by the power of a very skilled hypnotist and expert on mind control.

Again, be careful what you allow into your subconscious mind.

God's warning to the people of Israel also applies to us today:

> When you come into the land which the LORD your God is giving you, you shall not learn to follow the abominations of those nations. There shall not be found among you anyone who makes his son or his daughter pass through the fire, or one who practices witchcraft, or a soothsayer, or one who interprets omens, or a sorcerer, or one who conjures spells, or a medium, or a spiritist, or one who calls up the dead. For all who do these things are an abomination to the LORD, and because of these abominations the LORD your God drives them out from before you. You shall be blameless before the LORD your God (Deut. 18:9–13).

The New Age movement is growing very fast. Reincarnation is in vogue; it is self-salvation by coming back as another person until you get it right. Words like *harmonic vibrations, brotherhood,* and *world peace* are used. The leaders of the New Age movement talk of a one-world government, no cash, only credit cards, with everyone being given a number. They speak of control of the world food supply, the elimination of monotheistic religious people for purification of the world, so Christians, Jews, and Mohammedans would be exterminated (sounds very familiar). The sacred number is 666, which signifies worship of Lucifer. They say Christ has returned, but he is called Maitreya. He is *not* Jesus Christ.

The apostle Paul warns us in 1 Timothy 4:1–2: "Now the Spirit expressly says that in latter times some will depart from the faith, giving heed to deceiving spirits and doctrines of demons, speaking lies in hypocrisy, having their own conscience seared with a hot iron."

A prominent New Age spokesman, David Spangler, wrote in *Reflections of the Christ:* "Lucifer works within each of us to bring us to wholeness as we move into a new age, which is brought to that point which I term Luciferic initiation, the particular doorway through which the individual must pass if he is to come fully into the presence of his light and wholeness."[11]

Rebecca Brown, M.D., tells of listening to one of the spokespersons of the New Age movement, Benjamin Creme, in a meeting held in an Episcopal church in North Hollywood, California: "Throughout his talk he repeated the same theme: 'There are two major enemies of mankind—the United States of America and the fundamentalistic Christians.'" He stated that both must be brought to an end if the human race was to survive on planet earth. The audience clapped their approval.[12]

Maybe you haven't heard that there is a major war going on now, a spiritual war between the forces of God and Satan. The words of Paul are very true for today:

Finally, my brethren, be strong in the Lord and in the power of His might. Put on the whole armor of God, that you may be able to stand against the wiles of the devil. For we do not wrestle against flesh and blood, but against principalities, against powers, against the rulers of the darkness of this age, against spiritual hosts of wickedness in the heavenly places (Eph. 6:10–12).

I realize this is heavy spiritual medicine I am writing about. Maybe you would rather have me write on a more up-beat spiritual side of Christianity, such as that promoted by prosperity Christianity. But I have a hard time with that brand of self-centered Christianity, which makes God a celestial errand boy to bring wealth and prosperity to Christians. God has already given us the gift of His only begotten Son for our salvation. Prosperity Christianity, to parody the late President John F. Kennedy, says, "Ask not what you can do for God, but ask what God can do for you."

Maybe it's time to ask what God does want from us. First of all, God wants to be our only God: "You shall have no other gods before Me" (Deut. 5:7).

Today, we are confronted with the same serious decision about our lives and our relationship with God that confronted the people of Israel: "I have set before you life and death, blessing and cursing; therefore choose life, that both you and your descendants may live; that you may love the LORD your God, that you may obey His voice, and that you may cling to Him, for He is your life and the length of your days" (Deut. 30:19–20).

Jesus had some demanding things to say to people who want to follow Him and be His disciples: "No one can serve two masters; for either he will hate the one and love the other, or else he will be loyal to the one and despise the other. You cannot serve God and mammon" (Matt. 6:24); and "He who does not take his cross and follow after Me is not worthy of Me. He who finds his life will lose it, but he who loses his life for My sake will find it" (Matt. 10:38–39).

The call of discipleship is the call to obedience. Jesus said, "He who has My commandments and keeps them, it is he who loves Me. And he who loves Me will be loved by My Father, and I will love him and manifest Myself to him" (John 14:21).

I have come to the conclusion that if I am to be a follower of Jesus as my Lord and Master, I have to go all the way with my life and show my love by my obedience to Christ. Now for me to be spiritually alive and healthy means this type of commitment. It means more than spending an hour a week in church and praying only when I am in deep trouble. It means that I take seriously my spiritual life and growth.

Jesus said to Nicodemus and to you and me, "Unless one is born again, he cannot see the kingdom of God" (John 3:3).

Paul wrote, "If anyone is in Christ, he is a new creation; old things have passed away; behold, all things have become new" (2 Cor. 5:17). When a person is born again by the power of the Holy Spirit and becomes a Christian, he begins a new life. This is not the end of the growth of the spirit, but the beginning of the process of becoming a new person in Christ.

The process of becoming spiritually alive and healthy as a Christian is a pilgrimage, and each person is at a different place in that pilgrimage. Unfortunately for most of us, if you are like me, there are many starts and stops, times of wandering away from God and just living after the ways of the world.

I can tell you this. It is much easier to become religious than it is to become spiritual. I can be religious and try to follow all the rules and have beliefs and needs that express what I believe, but this is just head knowledge and not heart knowledge, which is truly experiencing the Spirit of God. I can be religious and spiritual at the same time—worshiping God in praise in a church service, confessing my faith in a creed, hearing God's Word, while also experiencing the presence of the Spirit of God.

The process of becoming a new person in Christ doesn't happen overnight. There was so much of the world's voices, morals, corruption, and pollution in my life that I didn't realize how conformed to the world as a Christian I had become.

The apostle Paul wrote,

> I beseech you therefore, brethren, by the mercies of God, that you present your bodies a living sacrifice, holy, acceptable to God, which is your reasonable service. And do not be conformed to this world, but be transformed by the renewing of your mind, that you may prove what is that good and acceptable and perfect will of God (Rom. 12:1–2).

Becoming a brand-new person means flushing out all the bitterness, resentment, and hates in one's life. It means no longer keeping score on persons who have hurt one. This new person is called to love as Jesus loves, but I can only love as Jesus loves if I yield to the Holy Spirit and receive the gift of love.

Instead of being so filled with love, I found out, as did the apostle Paul, that becoming spiritually a new creation is not easy. I keep messing up when I try to do what is right. Paul wrote,

> I delight in the law of God according to the inward man. But I see another law in my members, warring against the law of my mind, and bringing me into captivity to the law of sin which is in my members. O wretched man that I am! Who will deliver me from this body of death? I thank God—through Jesus Christ our Lord!" (Rom. 7:22–25).

John Wimber, founding pastor of Vineyard Ministries, says that "I first believed in Christ because I was not good, yet after becoming a Christian, I still struggled in my own strength with not being good enough. So I was always under conviction, always struggling with guilt." God spoke to him after he had cried out for help and said, "This issue is not being good, it is being God's."[13]

The old rebellious man of sin had to die before I could

belong to God. I did not realize how much I wanted to retain control of my life in my relationship with the Father. I fought surrendering my will and placing all my trust and faith in God to provide. In 1977 I began a serious spiritual pilgrimage to seek the will of God for my life.

At the beginning of my pilgrimage, I did not realize that God was calling me to live a life of holiness and obedience. I never considered myself to be holy, and I am sure those who know me very well, like family and friends, would never consider me to be holy. I began to realize the call to holiness was a call to know God and to experience His presence spiritually. In this process I die a little more each day to the flesh. It is a subtle process in which I may not be aware of how much I am changing, but when I look back, I realize that many things are no longer concerns in my life. For example, as a young man I had "new car fever" that hit me every spring, so I would trade in one car for another car. I now drive the car Jeannie's Dad and Mom owned before they died—a 1967 Chevrolet—and it is a wonderful car.

As I searched to know God, I realized how dry and empty I was spiritually, but I didn't even know how to become more spiritual. I prayed,

> O God, You are my God;
> Early will I seek You;
> My soul thirsts for You;
> My flesh longs for You
> In a dry and thirsty land
> Where there is no water (Ps. 63:1).

Since I live in the desert in Arizona, these words have a special meaning.

In Isaiah 55:6 I heard the truth of these words: "Seek the LORD while He may be found, call upon Him while He is near." I had always been able to accomplish what I set out to do in my life, and I assumed that my ideas and plans were in harmony with God's will. But I soon began to learn differently when I took seriously the desire to do what God wants for my life.

The words of Isaiah 55:8–9 pulled me up short:

"For My thoughts are not your thoughts,
Nor are your ways My ways," says the LORD.
"For as the heavens are higher than the earth,
So are My ways higher than your ways,
And My thoughts than your thoughts."

So when I realized how far away I was from knowing God and His plans and thoughts, I, in the spirit of our age, prayed to God for a "quick fix": "Okay, I have a lot of growing to do spiritually, so grow me up spiritually *now*. Well, maybe I can wait a few days until you fix me spiritually."

Apparently, God does not understand our "instant" society because my pilgrimage is taking a long time—and it is often a painful time. It is difficult to have my own plans and thoughts become subordinated to God's plan for me, but this is necessary in order to attain a more harmonious relationship with the Father.

I began to read the Bible as I had never read it before in my life. I realized there is a difference between reading the Word of God and God's speaking to me as the living Word of God. Paul Yonggi Cho writes, "People think they can believe in the Word of God. They can. But they fail to differentiate between the Word of God which gives general knowledge about God, and the Word of God which God uses to impart faith about specific circumstances into a man's heart. It is this latter type of faith which brings miracles."[14]

In the Greek language there are two different words for the Word of God. *Logos* is the general Word of God, about God. *Rhema* is the Word of God given to a specific person by the Holy Spirit. Romans 10:17 reveals that faith is more than just reading God's Word: "Faith comes by hearing, and hearing by the word of God." In this Scripture the "word" is not *logos* but *rhema*. Faith specifically comes by hearing the *rhema* Word of God, God speaking to me directly.

I found out that before I was to go out and do signs and wonders, God wanted me in close, intimate relationship with Him first. Of course I went out and tried to do signs and wonders, and when my doing wasn't working, I cried out to God, "Why, Lord? I pray for the sick, and nothing much happens!" In the silence that followed I searched the Scriptures and turned to Hosea 6:6: "I don't want your sacrifices—I want your love; I don't want your offerings—I want you to know me" (TLB).

It was finally dawning on me that God wants me to know, love, trust, and obey Him above all else in my life. It seems strange, but I believe He is much more concerned about my being totally His than with all the things I could do for the advancement of the kingdom of God here on earth. God wants me—all of me—to love Him with all my heart, mind, and soul.

For many Christians, their acceptance of Christ as their Savior and the empowering of the Holy Spirit are such mountaintop experiences that they are not prepared for the valleys that follow and the times in the wilderness. No one told me about the wilderness walk, which is a spiritual time of leanness, of trials and testing, of doubts and the silence of God.

The Israelites, after being delivered from their bondage in Egypt, went into the wilderness, not just geographically speaking, but to be spiritually tried and tested by God. I know some of you reading this chapter know firsthand what the wilderness experience is like because you are now walking through it or have walked through it at some time in your life.

I had always been successful, and I had been able to accomplish just about everything I set my mind to do. However, from 1984 to 1988, nothing I tried worked. I learned how to wait and wait and wait on the Lord. Apparently, my time and God's time are not the same, and God is insistent that things will be done in His time.

I prayed and prayed. I read the Bible as never before, hoping to hear from God. I found more trials and tests than ever before. I eagerly wanted to know and I wanted only to do the will of God, but how do you know the will of God when He is silent? Someone gave me these words written by Thomas Merton:

> Dear God,
>
> I have no idea where I am going. I do not see the road ahead of me. I cannot know for certain where it will end, nor do I really know myself, and the fact that I think that I am following your will does not mean that I am actually doing so. But I believe this. I believe that the desire to please you does in fact please you. I hope I have that desire in everything I do. I hope I never do anything apart from that desire, and I know that if I do this, you will lead me by the right road though I may know nothing about it at the time. Therefore I will trust you always though I may seem to be lost, and in the shadow of death. I will not be afraid because I know you will never leave me to face my troubles alone.[15]

My income from lecturing in dentistry dropped $40,000 in 1985. I tried to write a book, but God had taken his hand off me and my attempt failed. My clinical practice began to drop off, and I began to understand that what God wanted of me was to trust Him. I could really identify with the Israelites as they wandered in the wilderness for forty years: "And you shall remember that the LORD your God led you all the way these forty years in the wilderness, to humble you and test you, to know what was in your heart, whether you would keep His commandments or not" (Deut. 8:2).

I responded the same way the Israelites did with lots of murmuring against God. I had people praying for me during this time. One day an intercessor said she had a word from the Lord for me. I was thrilled! "What did the Lord say?" I asked eagerly. "He said that if you don't stop your murmuring, He will leave you in the wilderness." That did not cheer me up, but God made His point very clear to me.

Needless to say, the trials went on, and I was being tested as it says in 1 Peter 1:6–7: "You have been grieved by various trials, that the genuineness of your faith, being much more precious than gold that perishes, though it is tested by fire, may be found to praise, honor, and glory at the revelation of Jesus Christ."

I found it very hard to live out a faith walk by trusting the Father to provide everything for me. Now, I was not just going to sit back and say, "Okay, Father, provide for me." No, I was willing to work and earn my way if He would send the people for counseling. In June 1986, it was still a lean time financially. I didn't know how I would pay my office rent. So, for the umpteenth time I put my family, my home, my practice, everything I own and do on His altar, and said, "Lord, I surrender to You. I trust You to provide in all areas of my life." This was on a Tuesday. The next day I received a check for one hundred dollars as a memorial for a woman's husband who had died. I did not know the family, but I called and thanked the widow for the donation. I was surprised when she said, "I don't know who you are and what the Center for Living is. Maybe the check is from another family with the same name." I got her phone number off the check. Now you explain that one!

On Saturday of that week I stopped by to give private communion and pray for an eighty-year-old friend who was ill. Before I left, she said, "I want to give you a check for the Center for Living." It was for one hundred dollars.

On the following Tuesday I was to fly to Los Angeles to give an after-dinner speech. I arrived at the airport in plenty of time before my flight, so I bought a cold drink. Under the stool I noticed a bill—a hundred dollar bill. I was finally getting the message to put my trust in the Father to provide for me. I was learning to walk by faith, blind faith, one centered in God the Father to be my provider and my strength.

What is faith? "Faith is the substance of things hoped for, the evidence of things not seen" (Heb. 11:1).

I have come a long way in my spiritual pilgrimage. I am a child of God who knows, Abba Father, I belong to You. I love and obey Jesus. Thus, I am sent into this broken, wounded world of darkness to love and heal the sick, comfort those who mourn, set the captives free who are in bondage to Satan, love and care for the hungry, the naked, the poor, and the imprisoned.

The greatest living example of a spiritual life is Mother Teresa. She is God's love in action to the sick, the hungry, the homeless, the lepers, the dying, and the destitute. Mother Teresa said,

> The only thing that can remove poverty is sharing. Jesus came among the poorest, to teach people to love one another, which is to share, to use the gifts that God has given to people who have, to share with those who have not.
>
> But poverty is not just being without food. It is the absence of love. I can tell you there is more warmth in Calcutta, where people are willing to share what there is, than in many places where they have everything.[16]

In a speech in a cathedral at Delhi, she said,

People want to see Christ in others. Therefore we must love Christ with undivided love until it hurts. It must be a total surrender, a total conviction that nothing separates us from the love of Christ. We belong to Christ. There is so much love in us all, but we are often too shy to express our love and we keep it bottled up inside us. We must learn to love, to love until it hurts, and we will then know how to accept love.

We must be a channel of peace.

We must love until it hurts.

We must be Christ.

We must not be afraid to show our love.

India is recognizing the works of love, so too is the world. The Nobel Prize was awarded for love—is this not wonderful? If you love, then there is peace in your soul and joy in your heart.

Love God. Love God in the womb. Love God in the unborn child. Love God in the family. Love God in your neighbor. Love until it hurts.[17]

This is the secret of how spiritual health produces emotional, mental, and physical health and wellness.

NOTES

1. Viktor E. Frankl, *The Doctor and the Soul* (New York: Alfred A. Knopf, 1955).
2. Fritjot Capra, *The Turning Point* (New York: Simon & Schuster, 1982).
3. R. D. Laing, *The Voice of Experience* (New York: Pantheon, 1982).
4. James J. Lynch, *The Broken Heart* (New York: Basic Books, 1977).

5. Morton J. Kelsey, *Healing and Christianity* (New York: Harper & Row, 1973).

6. A. W. Tozer, *How to Be Filled with the Holy Spirit* (Harrisburg, Pa.: Christian Publications, 1928).

7. David Wilkerson, "The Cost of Going All the Way with God," *End-Times News Digest* (published by Omega Ministries, Medford, Oreg.), June 1988.

8. M. Scott Peck, *People of the Lie* (New York: Simon & Schuster, 1983).

9. Faye Fiore, "Speak of the Devil," *Scottsdale Progress,* Saturday Magazine, June 8, 1985.

10. Art Levine with Cynthis Kyle and Peter Dworkin, "Mystics on Main Street," *U.S. News & World Report,* February 8, 1987.

11. David Spangler, *Reflections of the Christ* (Scotland: Findhorn, 1977).

12. Rebecca Brown, *Prepare for War* (Chino, Calif.: Chick Publications, 1987).

13. John Wimber with Kevin Springer, *Power Evangelism* (San Francisco: Harper & Row, 1986).

14. Paul Yonggi Cho, *The Fourth Dimension* (Plainfield, N.J.: Logos International, 1979).

15. Thomas Merton, *Thoughts in Solitude* (New York: Farrar, Straus & Giroux, 1956).

16. Courtney Tower, "Mother Teresa's Work of Grace," *Reader's Digest,* December 1987.

17. Daphne Rae, *Love Until It Hurts* (San Francisco: Harper & Row, 1980).

CHAPTER NINE

IT'S ALL A MATTER OF STYLE—LIFE-STYLE

There are no quick, easy fixes in the art of staying well in an uptight world. The tensions in the world are in a state of constant flux and threat. The ability to adapt to all the stress, changes, tensions, and fears is up to each individual. The time is past when you can give all the responsibility for your health and healing to your physician. That may be the easier way, but it is not how to stay well. In fact, have you ever gone to your physician when you were well and asked for a plan for a life-style of positive wellness?

I just love the story Dr. John C. McCamy tells of the time he asked a group of college students to go to the health center of their university to find out what would happen if healthy people asked for health care from a physician. These four students were healthy, energetic, and vigorous.

The students explained to the physician that they were completely well and had no complaints. Since this was a health center, they wanted advice on how to stay well.

The first student was taken behind a curtain, and the doctor told him in sympathetic and confidential tones, "It's all right. Our records are private. You can just tell me about your disease. No one else will ever know."

"But I don't have a disease," the student said. "I'm well."

"Yes, I know," reasoned the doctor. "We won't tell your parents, the dean, or anybody else. We'll give you a shot of penicillin."

"I don't have a venereal disease," persisted the student, "or anything else."

The first student was not treated for venereal disease, nor were he and his friends told how to stay well, but he was referred to a psychiatrist. If he did not have a physical disease, then he obviously had a mental disorder.[1]

The art of staying well requires you to develop a personal life-style in which you accept the responsibility for your own good health—learning and developing new ways of healthy living as well as eliminating destructive behaviors that undermine your health and prepare you for illness and death. The breaking of destructive habit patterns and replacing them with new healthy patterns is hard work. It is a commitment to change your life-style, even though this may be difficult.

You are the expert on you because no one else in the world knows you as well as you know yourself; therefore, I want you to examine your life and identify what destructive behaviors undermine your health and what positive changes you can make for a life-style of positive wellness.

Is one of your destructive behaviors smoking cigarettes or using other forms of tobacco? When I was a child, I often heard older people call cigarettes "coffin nails." Little did they realize how accurate was that nickname.

Smoking tobacco is blamed for *one thousand deaths per day* in our country. Most lung cancer could be prevented by simply not smoking tobacco. I don't understand how our federal government can spend billions of dollars in a war on cancer, labeling cigarette packages with the surgeon general's warning that cigarette smoking may be hazardous to your health, and then turn around and give taxpayers' money to subsidize the farmers who grow the tobacco. It is as absurd as our federal government subsidizing a group of terrorists in our country with massive amounts of money resulting in the killing of an average of one thousand U.S. citizens a day.

Not only does depression make a person smoking tobacco a more likely candidate for lung cancer, but now research is discovering that the killer T cells of our immune system are made impotent by cigarette smoke. Killer T cells latch onto invading cancer cells and literally punch holes in them to destroy them. Smokers suppress the production of killer T cells five to six times the rate of nonsmokers. Killer T cells cannot function properly in lungs polluted with smoke.[2]

How hard is it to quit smoking? It is a real battle, but people are quitting smoking in record numbers. It is estimated that between thirty-five million and forty million Americans have quit smoking since 1964. About 95 percent of Americans who have stopped smoking did so without hypnosis, drugs, group treatment, or help of any kind, so if you smoke, there is hope that you can quit, too.[3] Don't get discouraged if you try and fail. Analyze your failure to see what caused it.

I smoked for twenty years, and I was always quitting as evidenced by the fact that I never purchased a carton of cigarettes. What a waste of money—all those unsmoked packages of cigarettes! There were times I really did quit, like when I was very sick with the flu. For a few weeks after recovering, I did not smoke again until I bummed a cigarette from a friend. I was smoking again, only I wasn't buying, just smoking "other people's" cigarettes. I soon realized that I would look at the list of people I would see in therapy that particular day, and I knew which ones smoked and what brands. I could smoke "O.P.'s" cigarettes that day! Then I would notice cigarette machines calling me by name, but I was confident that I would buy just one pack of cigarettes, so my money would once again be inserted into the machine. Thus, I was back to smoking at the same rate I was before I got the flu, but I was determined not to buy a carton—because I was quitting!

In 1969, I was invited to Maui, Hawaii, to help teach a seminar to dentists and their wives. We stayed at beautiful Napili Bay. There is a nice reef not too far offshore, so I put on my fins and snorkeling mask and swam out there. I was huffing and puffing so badly I really struggled to make it to the reef. That really shook me up because I am an ex-football player and boxer. My self-image as an athlete was devastated. But I still continued to smoke.

During these years, I was working in an outpatient drug treatment center I had started for teenagers. It became very hypocritical of me to tell kids to stop using dope because it was addictive and dangerous to health. Often a teenager would say to me, "Tell us all about it, Doc. You've been an addict longer than most of us have been alive." Of course I was smoking and coughing, and I was nailed by the truth.

I had a staff of five ex-addicts who also felt moved to quit smoking. In the evening before the group broke up into small groups, we had a time for commitments to be made before the group. If a person made a commitment to stop smoking, as the staff members did, then a penalty was agreed upon if that person broke the commitment. All five of the male ex-addicts had long hair, so as each one made his commitment to quit smoking, he accepted the penalty of shaving his head if he broke the commitment, even if it was just one cigarette.

Well, I was already on my way to that state of baldness so I had to promise to give two hundred dollars to the American Cancer Society if I broke my commitment.

I quit in October 1970, and I have never had another cigarette. The next year when I went to Maui, Hawaii, to teach in another seminar, I was overjoyed to be able to swim out to the reef with no effort, and I also swam around Puna Point into an adjoining bay. I had restored my lungs. The cup of tobacco tar in each lung was gone. You couldn't pay me $1 million to smoke cigarettes again. My mouth felt clean, my breath was not of stale smoke, and my hair and my clothes no longer had the smell of stale tobacco smoke. It was great to be free of the addiction to tobacco.

I learned one very important thing that made the difference in never smoking another cigarette. I realized that I had twenty years of stored memories of smoking in my subconscious mind and that one cigarette was not just one cigarette, but the "on" button to memories of smoking. I made a decision to never push that "on" button again, and I made the decision that I would not fall into the trap of self-pity because I was not able to smoke. When I had quit before, I pushed the "on" button with one cigarette, which triggered the memories of smoking. Those memories soon took over, so before long I was smoking as much as I did before I quit.

If you are a heavy smoker and want to quit, first develop good nutritional habits and take multivitamins with additional vitamin C. You must begin to give your body energy from food, and not the too-typical "breakfast" of coffee and cigarettes. Don't try to quit smoking when you are under a great deal of stress. Wait until your life is more in balance and you have more normal energy levels.

I suggest that people who want to quit smoking should take 10,000 mg of vitamin C, time released, because vitamin C is a potent detoxifier that counteracts and neutralizes the harmful effects of many poisons in the body. It will combat various inorganic poisons, such as mercury and arsenic. Ascorbic acid (vitamin C) neutralizes the bad reactions of many organic poisons, drugs, bacterial and animal toxins, and it also detoxifies carbon monoxide, sulfur dioxide, and carcinogens. Ascorbic acid is the only immediate protection we have against the bad effects of air pollution and smoking.[4]

In the Old West, when you went into a bar, the bartender would ask you to name your "poison." The truth is that alcohol is a poison that must be broken down metabolically by the liver to make it a less harmful substance. If the liver is overworked in the breaking down of alcohol, there is resultant protein depletion, causing atrophy and impairment of liver functions.

A recent report in *The Arizona Republic,* "Liquor Hurts the Immune System," states that though the liver suffers more than the other organs, they, too, may suffer damage: "Brain cells are altered and many die. Memory formation is blocked, and the senses are dulled. In the long term, irreversible damage occurs. Physical coordination is impaired."

The article goes on to say that alcohol can cause deterioration of the heart muscle, may trigger bleeding in stomach and intestines, and affects the immune system since it keeps infection-fighting cells from functioning properly, causing increased risk of viral or bacterial disease.

Alcohol may affect the reproduction system. In men, hormone levels can be changed resulting in a lower sex drive; in women, menstrual cycles can become irregular, and ovaries may malfunction. Pregnant women risk bearing children with birth defects.

The debilitating effects of alcohol on the immune system may help explain the drug's devastating effect on many heavy drinkers, according to recent research conducted at the University of Arizona and elsewhere.

The effects of chronic alcohol use on the disease-fighting cells of the immune system may explain why alcoholics have high rates of cancer, pneumonia, tuberculosis, cholera, hepatitis and liver damage, said Dr. Ronald Watson, head of an inter-departmental alcohol-research effort for the U.A.

The numbers of key immune-system cells decreased by about one-third in heavy drinkers in another study conducted by Watson and his colleagues. About 30 heavy drinkers were compared with both former drinkers and a group of Mormons who said they had never drunk. The immune systems of the heavy drinkers were heavily affected, and those of the people who had stopped drinking were less strongly affected.[5]

Now medical researchers are warning that alcohol and tobacco do not mix. In fact, at times these two substances act synergistically by making each other more powerful and causing more damage than either would have alone. Some researchers believe that 76 percent of the cases of oral cancer and cancer of the esophagus are caused by simultaneous exposure to tobacco and alcohol.[6]

Alcohol abuse is the number one drug abuse problem in the United States, even though we tend to separate alcohol from other drugs of addiction. The leaders of our government in Washington, D.C., want the people in America to say no to drugs; but one gets the feeling that alcohol isn't included. Maybe alcohol addiction strikes too close to home to call it a drug since Washington, D.C., has the highest rate of alcoholism in the country.

In the late sixties and early seventies I spent a lot of time giving speeches on drug abuse and developing treatment centers for drug abusers in the Valley of the Sun. It wasn't until after NBC filmed a documentary on drug abuse in America that people in Arizona began to take the drug problem seriously and raise money for a staffing grant. About one-half of NBC's white paper, "Trip to Nowhere," was filmed about programs we were developing in Phoenix. It became "in" to do something about drug abuse. In fact, one of the most prominent people in Arizona hosted a cocktail party to raise money for drug abuse. I will never forget one woman who told me, a bit tipsily, that she was so worried about the drug problem that she didn't know what she would do without her Valium and Librium. I did agree that the drug problem was more serious than most people believed.

The destructiveness of alcoholism is impossible to measure in the lives of those who are physically destroyed, the loved ones who are wounded emotionally as well as physically. Alcohol is a factor in nearly half of America's murders, suicides, and accidental deaths. Alcoholism claims at least 100,000 lives per year, which is *twenty-five times* as many lives claimed by all illegal drugs combined. The economic costs of alcoholism and alcohol abuse are estimated at nearly *$117 billion* a year.[7] Now that's a lot of money!

The next part of your life-style to consider is your sex life. One of the most destructive areas of the American life-style has to do with the practice of casual sexual relationships. The United States has worked hard to become a sexually liberated nation through millions of books to help us achieve more enjoyment from our sex lives and through the development of sex therapy to help people overcome their hang-ups in their sex lives. Movies and television programs have become more and more sexually explicit, and sexual morality has been systematically disqualified and mocked in the process. The result of this sexual liberation and the relentless search for more "joy of sex" has been disastrous. As a nation, we have sown the wind and reaped a whirlwind (see Hos. 8:7).

The deadly epidemic of AIDS grows daily along with an epidemic of other sexually transmitted diseases. According to the federal Centers for Disease Control in Atlanta, Georgia, this nation is in the midst of an epidemic of sexually transmitted diseases that infect an average of thirty-three thousand people a day. At this rate, one in four Americans between the ages of fifteen and fifty-five will eventually suffer from a sexually transmitted disease. Not only has a much stronger form of syphilis appeared, but millions are suffering from a painful infection that even doctors, until recent years, had never heard of—Chlamydia, which carries risks of infertility and problems during pregnancy.[8]

Casual sex has proven very costly. The joy of sex has been replaced by the fear of promiscuous sex and a return to monogamous sexual relationships.

The next area that is a hazard to the art of staying well is the toxic world we live in, outdoors as well as indoors. When I began doing my research into this area, I became more and more depressed, and I wondered why I was still alive. I am not the only person who believes that there has been too much sensationalism by the media and not enough scientific research before we worry and frighten everyone to death.

I love to go to baseball games once in a while, and a real treat for me has been to have a hot dog, but now I worry about the possible cancer risks from eating nitrites in the hot dog. My wife colors her hair to hide the gray, but then I read an article that said hair dye could cause cancer, so I worried about her getting cancer.

I also became depressed when I read an article entitled "Living May Be Hazardous to Your Health." The alternative to living is not too appealing to me. The article reported that the Environmental Protection Agency (EPA) says that eighty-three of the largest cities in the United States have chemically contaminated water supplies. Although most of the water is safe from bacteria, it is not safe chemically.[9]

The beautiful Valley of the Sun in which I live is now the Valley of the Smog, which can't be very healthy to breathe each day. Lead from gasoline does cause cancer, so finally the lead is being removed from it. And rain from polluted skies kills forests and fish in lakes and streams. Do you see what I mean about becoming depressed about this toxic world?

While I was worried about outdoor pollution, pesticides, and all those other things, President Carter asked us to seal doors and windows in order to conserve energy. But sealing houses and workplaces caused indoor pollution, a much more serious hazard to health than outdoor pollution. Where is a person to go to feel safe from this toxic world?

Every day in our homes and offices we are bombarded with pollutants, contaminants, pesticides, chemicals in cleaning agents, smoke fumes from gas stoves and wood stoves, food additives—well, it's a wonder any of us are still alive. Remember in 1976 how a contaminated air conditioning system in a Philadelphia hotel led to the death of thirty-four American Legionnaires?

Have you ever noticed how many new office buildings are all glass but are hermetically sealed to reduce energy costs of refrigeration and heating? People get sick from working in these buildings. These illnesses can reduce productivity and increase absenteeism. The solution? A breath of fresh air, in fact, lots of fresh air.

On September 12, 1988, the EPA and the surgeon general's office urged America's homeowners to test their houses for the presence of radioactive radon gas. Radon is an odorless, colorless gas resulting from the radioactive decay of radium. It may also happen as a result of fumes from common building materials, cleaners, and solvent materials kept inside a building or in a home. Radon is the second leading cause of lung cancer, right after smoking. The EPA has estimated that radon accounts for 20,000 of the nation's 130,000 annual lung cancer deaths. Surgeon General C. Everett Koop said it is especially important to warn people about the deadly combination of smoking and radon that can multiply an individual's risk of lung cancer by fifteen times or more.

Now before a person buys a home, there should be not only a termite inspection report, but also a radon level content report. The cost of testing a home is only fifteen to twenty dollars. The best solution is to bring in fresh air; air out houses and other buildings.[10]

What is the answer to living in this toxic world? Simple!

1. Don't drink the water.
2. Don't breathe the air—indoors or outdoors.

The surgeon general's report on nutrition and health, which was released in 1988, calls for us to replace foods high in fat or cholesterol with vegetables, fruit, whole grains, fish, poultry, lean meat, and low-fat dairy products. The surgeon general says, "If you don't smoke or drink excessively, your diet can influence your long term health prospects more than any other action you might take.[11]

In regard to your weight and wellness, I shall spare giving you the latest fad diet to lose weight. I have noticed that fad diets are good for selling books and making money for the authors, but most weight lost on a fad diet is soon regained.

Losing weight and keeping it off is a matter of making good decisions about what foods you know you need to eliminate or severely restrict and what foods are healthy for you. I will give one helpful hint: If there is a food you crave, such as chocolate, you most likely have a hidden food allergy or addiction. Unfortunately, the most common hidden allergies are to the most commonly eaten foods, such as coffee, corn, wheat, eggs, milk, yeast, beef, and pork. In fact, any food can cause an allergic reaction.[12]

A Roman Catholic priest shared the story of his addiction to chocolate. He said that if he got his hands on a two-pound box of chocolates, he would not stop eating until the candy was all gone. People in his parish had sent him seventy-eight pounds of chocolate for the past Christmas, and his secretary quickly gave it away to charitable organizations.

I would also like to add a word to the wise about developing a healthy life-style. Don't become so obsessed with having the body beautiful that you are never satisfied or happy. Having the "perfect body" has become a neurotic illness for many people, especially women, who become anorexics, "the death camp look," or bulimics who live a life consumed with "scarfing and barfing."

A life-style of positive wellness for me means that because I am now fifty-eight years old, I shouldn't feel guilty because I don't look like the trim, muscular athlete I was in college. After all, the good life is more than a piece of dry whole wheat toast, grapefruit, and smelly gym suits.

Developing a healthy life-style is more than just eliminating destructive behaviors. There is one very important foundation for a life of positive wellness, and that is for you to come to terms with answering the question, What am I living for? A table, a chair, a plate, a knife, and a fork know what they are for. What are you for? Is it worth living for? Is it worth dying for?

I was deeply moved when I read Viktor Frankl's account of his survival in the death camp at Auschwitz in *Man's Search For Meaning*. He quoted the philosopher Nietzsche's words as very meaningful to him: "He who has a why to live can bear with almost any how." Frankl reported that those prisoners with a deep spiritual life survived better than those who did not have a spiritual core to their being, even if they were physically stronger.

Frankl wrote,

Even though conditions such as lack of sleep, insufficient food, and various mental stress may suggest that the inmates were bound to react in certain ways, in the final analysis it became clear that the sort of person the prisoner became was the result of an inner decision and not the result of camp influences alone. Fundamentally, therefore, any man can, even under such circumstances, decide what shall become of him—mentally and spiritually. He may retain his human dignity even in a concentration camp.[13]

Ever since I first saw the horrible pictures of the death camps with dead bodies stacked up like cords of wood, I was tormented by nightmares of the Holocaust. Ten million people so sadistically destroyed! My wife, Jeannie, and I have visited the death camp of Dachau. I have asked myself, "If I had been a prisoner in Dachau, what would my inner decision have been? Would I have thrown myself into the electrified fence to put an end to my misery, or would I have chosen to live beyond the death camp to give something back to life?" I don't know what my inner decision would have been.

The inner decisions you make about your priorities in life, your values, what you are living for, form your personal philosophy of life. How you are living your life is the result of your belief system or philosophy of life, whether you have verbalized it or not.

If money, self-gratification, status, power, buying bigger and more expensive toys, greed, or work is the priority of your life, then that is the why of your life. If your life is driven by a compulsive spirit of competition, then it is also manifest in your work and play. Competition and winning are as American as apple pie. The Lombardi credo is prevalent across the land: "Winning isn't everything. It's the only thing." This credo teaches life by comparison and one-upmanship. A person can win only by making the other person look bad. Such competitiveness breeds anxiety, distrust of others, and loneliness.

From a poem I wrote, "How Do I Destroy Myself? Let Me Count The Ways," are these words:

I have a rendezvous with success
I rush and frantically push
My body to extreme distress.
These words echo in my mind—
Compete, compete, and never retreat.
Strive for the best, so fast my heart
Does beat.
Be perfect, no less; then one day
I will have success.
But lost in the din is the voice
Within crying,
Stop! Be wise. Is this the life you
Prize?
A collection of things gathered
While rushing to die, but
Never finding out the "why?"[14]

If you want a simple way to help identify what you are living for, just write your own obituary of what will be said about your life.

Raymond Moody, M.D., who wrote *Life After Life* and *Reflections on Life After Life,* interviewed hundreds of people who had near death experiences. He asked them to talk about what happened before they were brought back to life, during the time their spirits were gone from their bodies. Most individuals reported an encounter with God, or with a being of very bright light, who asked probing, nonverbal questions followed by panoramic views of their lives shown with startling intensity. They saw for themselves how their lives had affected other people, and they judged their own lives. Among the questions asked was a powerful yet simple one, provocative and haunting, "Whom have you loved?"[15] How would you answer that question?

The key to having a life of positive wellness is having a life of balance. For example, there have been times when my life has been out of balance because of workaholic behavior, which caused my family life to suffer. Similarly, because of the high cost of living and materialistic goals, fifty percent of mothers work full-time jobs, which causes children and family life to suffer. I believe it is critical to the strength of our country that family life be given top priority.

Jesus said, "For what will it profit a man if he gains the whole world, and loses his own soul? Or what will a man give in exchange for his soul?" (Mark 8:36–37). What will it profit a family if it has the newest cars and all the latest things yet loses its children to drugs, delinquency, and emotional problems?

What value do we place on family life? Healthy, loving families produce healthy, loving people. An ever-growing curiosity for life and learning is necessary for a balanced life. The driving learning force in babies is curiosity to learn, and children learn because learning satisfies that need to grow and feels good inside. There are so many things I have yet to learn that I've decided I won't have time to die—there will always be one more thing I've yet to learn or to try.

People do not suffer as much from hardening of the arteries as from hardening of the attitudes. The brain, like our muscles, must be used so there will be no atrophy.

At the center of the balance for my life is Jesus Christ, my Lord and Savior. I have decided to "seek first the kingdom of God and His righteousness, and all these things shall be added to [me]" (Matt. 6:33).

It takes a lot of faith in God to not be anxious and to not

worry about the day-to-day struggle to live. But once you learn to keep your eyes on God instead of on the circumstances in your life, you can let God be the Lord of your life and the power for your life through the Holy Spirit. You can experience the release of not having to do everything in your own power and strength.

The apostle Paul had more than his share of suffering, beatings, stonings, and imprisonments, yet he could write these words from jail:

> Rejoice in the Lord always. Again I will say, rejoice! Let your gentleness be known to all men. The Lord is at hand. Be anxious for nothing, but in everything by prayer and supplication, with thanksgiving, let your requests be made known to God; and the peace of God, which surpasses all understanding, will guard your hearts and minds through Christ Jesus (Phil. 4:4–7).

It is exciting to discover how faith in Jesus Christ to be Lord of my life frees me from anxiety about life, gives me a spirit of love, peace, and thanksgiving instead of an attitude of bitterness, inner turmoil, and self-pity. I also don't need to play the role of judge over other people's lives. I can leave that to God.

Not only does each person whistle through his own beak and sing his own song, but each person sees his world through his own eyes. What he sees and responds to is determined by what he believes about himself, people, and the world. Each person looks at life through a different vision. Three men can look at a tree. One man will see so many feet of valuable lumber worth so much money. The second man will see it as so much firewood to be burned to keep his family warm in the winter. The third man will see it as a masterpiece of God's creative art, given to man as an expression of God's love and enduring strength, with a value far beyond its worth in money or firewood. What we live for determines what we see in life and gives clear focus to our inner vision.[16]

I'll never forget a book I read in my senior year of high school called *Omnibus* by David Grayson. I can't remember what the story was about, but I'll never forget the simple philosophy of life expressed by a Swedish blacksmith in a small country town. Someone asked him why he never said an unkind word or gossiped about anyone else. He replied, "When I begin to think about somebody else's faults, I just begin with myself and I never get any further." I would really like to know someone like that—and I would like to be like that village blacksmith.

That story reminded me of the time a woman was caught in adultery and was about to be stoned to death in accordance with Mosaic law. The Pharisees sought to trap Jesus by asking Him what they should do, and Jesus simply said to them, "He who is without sin among you, let him throw a stone at her first" (John 8:7).

One by one the crowd melted away until only Jesus and the woman remained. Jesus asked her, "Woman, where are those accusers of yours? Has no one condemned you?" "No one, Lord," she replied. Jesus said, "Neither do I condemn you; go and sin no more" (John 8:10–11).

I think you realize that the art of staying well has no quick fixes because it demands the development of a healthy life-style in which each person develops an individual philosophy of life. You must ask yourself, What am I living for? What is the purpose of my life? You must constantly reevaluate your priorities in life, looking at what is driving you. Is it worth dying for? You must also ask, How long do I want to live? How do I want to live the rest of my life?

The most priceless possession you have is your health. If you were worth $1 billion but were paralyzed with a stroke, you would jump at the chance to trade places with a person who had no money but had his health.

If you decide to make the art of staying well in an uptight world your goal, remember, you will not reach that goal overnight. There is an old Chinese proverb that says, "The longest journey begins with a single step." If you make that decision, take that step. You will be on the journey to health. Where you start and how fast you travel on your journey to positive wellness is up to you. If you backslide, don't be discouraged. Just get back on the road again.

The basic question is this: Health or sickness, which do you choose?

NOTES

1. John C. McCamy and James Presley, *Human Life Styling* (New York: Harper & Row, 1975).
2. David Weissman, "Smoke Kills Cells Aimed at Invaders," Address delivered at the 81st Annual American Lung Association, Anaheim, California, May 13, 1985.
3. James F. Sallis, "A Guide to Quitting Smoking on Your Own," *Executive Health Report* 24 (March 1988).
4. Irwin Stone, *The Healing Factor* (New York: Grossett & Dunlap, 1972).
5. Peter Aleshine, "Liquor Hunts Immune System," *The Arizona Republic,* October 16, 1988.
6. Lowell Ponte, "Deadly Mixers: Alcohol and Tobacco," *Reader's Digest,* April 1985.
7. Lewis J. Lord with Erica Goode, Ted Gert, Kathleen Mcauliffe, Lisa J. Moore, Robert F. Black, Nancy Linnon, and Bureau Reports, "Coming to Grips with Alcoholism," *U.S. News & World Report,* November 30, 1987.
8. Lewis J. Lord with Jeannye Thornton, Joseph Carey, and the

Domestic Bureau, "Sex with Care," *U.S. News & World Report,* June 2, 1986.

9. Gillian Conneley, "Living May Be Hazardous to Your Health," *American Way Magazine,* February 1980.

10. Betty Beard, "Homeowners Urged to Run Radon Check," *The Arizona Republic,* September 13, 1988.

11. Joanne Silberner, "A Call to Get the Fat Out," *U.S. News & World Report,* August 8, 1988.

12. Theron G. Randolph and Ralph W. Mors, *Alternative Approach to Allergies* (New York: Bantam Books, 1982).

13. Viktor E. Frankl, *Man's Search for Meaning* (New York: Washington Square Press, 1963).

14. Ken Olson, *Can You Wait Till Friday?* (Phoenix: O'Sullivan-Woodside, 1975).

15. Personal conversation with Raymond A. Moody, Jr.

16. Olson, Ibid.